GIVING GOD'S WAY

PUBLISHED by Mike LaBahn & Associates
CONTRIBUTING EDITS by Jenny Pedersen
SPECIAL THANKS to Kathryn Belsey, Michael Wourms & Wesley Fulkerson
BOOK DESIGN by Troy Hollinger

4616 Calavo Drive
La Mesa, CA 91941

mikelabahn.com

ISBN 978-0-9910043-2-4

TO MY

WIFE

CHILDREN

GRAND CHILDREN

GREAT GRAND CHILDREN

GREAT GREAT GRAND CHILDREN

Some years ago I did some soul searching and took an inventory of my spiritual life. I felt that I needed a challenge that would spur me on in spiritual growth. I could look back and see how God had brought growth and maturity in many areas of my life and ministry and was deeply grateful for His grace. But it was clear there was an area that lagged behind.

Although I had always tithed cheerfully and given offerings when there was a need, I knew people who gave with a liberality and joy that was unknown to me. I marveled at their great generosity and the freedom and joy with which they gave. On the other hand, I tended to give with a conservative caution and I was always happy when someone else picked up the check. What did these people know that I didn't?

I felt Jesus was calling me to follow Him into a new adventure. I prayed and asked that God would enlarge my heart & make me a generous giver. I was excited by the prospect of spiritual growth and a new level of partnership with Him.

I made a fresh dedication of all that I had to Him. I repented of sometimes being a reluctant giver. Almost immediately God presented me with opportunities to give and began me on a journey of discovering the great joy of giving. I began to give with a freedom and joy I had never known before. One day, I realized that I loved to give. The more I gave the happier I was. Amazingly the more I gave the more I seemed to have. Even when I gave sacrificially it seemed like I continued to prosper even more. God was providing more so I could give more.

Like every other area of spiritual growth in my life it came as a result of studying God's Word, facing and overcoming fears and wrong attitudes in my life, but most of all trusting in God's grace. I look back with real joy as I see how God had transformed me. My attitude toward money and possessions changed and I am happier for it.

Mike LaBahn was one of those generous and cheerful givers who inspired me. Together with others he modeled the joy of giving with great generosity. He lived out Jesus' words, "It is more blessed to give than to receive" Acts 20:35. I have personally witnessed Mike and Julie's generosity to others and have seen the growth in God's Kingdom through their giving.

While still a very young couple with very little money, Mike and Julie felt called to a lifestyle of generous giving and set a giving goal that must have seemed unreasonable, if not impossible, to anyone they told. In this book Mike takes us on a wonderful tour of how God brought these desires and goals into reality.

Mike has spent his adult life both in giving and also in studying about giving. In these pages Mike shares what he has learned with us. This book is very readable and full of wonderful and inspiring illustrations from Mike's life as well as the lives of others. A book of this nature is both needed and welcome. As one who has learned the joy of giving, I heartily encourage you to join in this adventure. You couldn't have a better guide than Mike LaBahn.

FOREWORD - **Mark Hoffman**

INTRODUCTION
OUR GIVING STORY
15

Chapter 1 - **WHAT IS BIBLICAL GIVING?** **35**

Chapter 2 - **WHY GIVE?**
THE CALL TO HONOR GOD
55

Chapter 3 - **BENEFITS OF GIVING**
THE DIVIDENDS OF GOD
69

Chapter 4 - **WHY WE DO NOT GIVE** **79**

Chapter 5 - **GREED** **91**

Chapter 6 - **WHEN WE FORGET GOD** **101**

Chapter 7 - **GIVING PATTERNS**
FROM THE BIBLE
113

Chapter 8 - **HOW NOT TO GIVE**
PATTERNS IN THE BIBLE
157

Chapter 9 - **OVERCOMING OBSTACLES** **171**

CONCLUSION **185**

GIVING GOD'S WAY

RADICAL GENEROSITY WILL CHANGE YOUR LIFE

MIKELaBAHN

What's the first thing you think when you sit down to hear a sermon and you discover it's going to be about tithing? What about when a friend recommends that you read a book on giving? If you're anything like most people, your first response might be to feel a little apprehensive or overwhelmed. Some people even feel resentful, as if they already know they'll be conned or forced to do something against their will.

If your arm needs twisting in order to get you to give, this is a sign of spiritual sickness. Although they may not be used to the idea in the beginning, spiritually healthy people want to give. Because they are so thankful for what their Father in heaven has freely given them, it is hard to stop growing Christians from giving! Have you heard or made these excuses for not giving?

"I've worked hard for my money; it's mine!"
"I already give to charities in my community; why do I also have to give to the church?"
"I designate my giving instead of tithing. It's pretty much the same thing."
"Tithing is just Old Testament legalism."
"The Holy Spirit prompts me when and where to give."

These excuses sound silly when compared with Scripture. The Psalmist declares, *"The earth is the LORD'S, and all it contains, the world, and those who dwell in it"* Psalm 24:1. *"For every beast of the forest is Mine, the cattle on a thousand hills...and everything that moves in the field is Mine"* Psalm 50:10-11. Sometimes we need a reminder that the principles outlined in the Bible for Christian giving are not for God's benefit but for ours.

Our Giving Story

When we were married on Saturday, August 12, 1978, it seemed to always be a struggle to keep gas in our tank. Our car ran on fumes. At the time, neither of us realized our relationship with each other was completely void of the spiritual fuel we needed to make a marriage function; we soon discovered that we too were running on fumes.

We both came from rag-tag, fractured backgrounds...broke and broken. Julie left a home absent of her father when she was a young teenager of sixteen and managed to earn enough money to support her own apartment and purchase a car. I came from a fatherless home, was kicked out of my house while still in high school, then left to somehow make it on my own. We were birthed in dysfunctional families, raised in poverty, taught bad habits, and never given any instructions on how to handle money. When I was a young boy, I remember feeling so embarrassed because I did not have even 25 cents in change to buy a simple Coke. I vowed to myself, "I will NOT raise my family like this!"

We were two young people with relationship voids the size of a large moon crater, but we did the best we could from what we knew at the time. Julie worked odd jobs while attending nursing school, and with the dogged determination of youth, ultimately earned her LVN degree. I worked at Aunt Emma's as a fry cook, and did side jobs cleaning the brush for fire prevention. "We had a terrible background," Julie observes. "Sometimes it felt like a bad toothache...you always know it is there, and when you put pressure on it, it hurts even more!"

We both became Christians early on in our marriage and began to submit ourselves to the process of studying God's Word and centering our lives and marriage on His principles.

A PLAID COUCH AND A BEAST

We owned a plaid couch in the living room that badly needed replacing. The seats on the couch were permanently attached to the frame and could not be removed. As the fabric became worn, the springs in the seats started to pop up and poke people when they sat down. Eventually, the pillows flattened out, the stitching broke, the plaid pattern faded, and the couch started to unravel. "Honestly, that couch was uncomfortable and embarrassing," Julie remembers. Three times we tried to save up money to purchase a new couch, but each time our fledgling business had a financial need that became the top priority.

Our family car was affectionately known as the Brown Beast. The two-tone, beige and yellow, tin-paneled station wagon could be heard clanking its way down the street before it was seen sending up smoke signals. The wagon also had a particularly annoying, unpredictable habit of locking us in or out at will because of a short in the electrical system. These family lock outs were entirely without warning, and extremely inconvenient, especially when Julie was trying to transport kids around to school or other activities. One time, on a much-needed, long-overdue family vacation, the engine of the family station wagon fell out when the motor mounts snapped! "There were days," Julie remembers, "when we felt like we would never break free of breakdowns and being broke."

We needed to do something to begin to get our finances and our life under control. One of our first steps was to become Christians and to start attending church. Our first pastor, Robin Hadfield, said something that changed our financial life and has guided our financial journey ever since: "If God can go through you with money, He will." Although we were new Christians, we started to learn about biblical, financial principles, and then we learned about tithing (giving 10 percent of our income to God). We simply declared, "We need to do whatever God's Word tells us to do," and Malachi 3:10 NKJV was clear to us:

Bring all the tithes into the storehouse, that there may be food in My house, and try Me now in this," says the Lord of hosts, "if I will not open for you the windows of heaven and pour out for you such blessing that there will not be room enough to receive it."

We decided we would not be simply Christians who tithed; because we both came from such lack in our lives, we wanted to be givers. We embraced the words of Jesus when He said, *"It is more blessed to give than to receive"*. (Acts 20:35) It became our goal to give more than our tithe regardless of how little money we were making. Although we did not have much to give, we gave what we had. Every time we gave, it required sacrifice.

SMALL STEPS, BIG CHALLENGES

Before we started our business, both of us worked at two fulltime jobs for two years to save enough money to help support ourselves as we began our own business. We had no business experience, little education, marginal skills, and very meager capital. What we did have was a willingness to work hard, a desire to be self-employed, and a sincere earnestness to help others.

We started LaBahn's Landscaping in 1981 with a rather limited vision - mow lawns for money. Our business plan seemed simple: "The more lawns we mow, the more income we can generate." Because neither of us knew much about how to handle or budget money, we always seemed to be under immense financial pressure. We were so poor we could not even replace the starter in our company truck. With Julie in the cab and me pushing the truck, she would pop the clutch to get us started so we could go from one job to another.

One of the jobs we performed besides mowing lawns was to create fire prevention "safe zones" for clients by clearing off their lots of brush and weeds. Julie, standing barely 5' tall, became an amazing helper, even driving the truck to the dump and single-handedly unloading the heavy branches and dusty brush by herself!

As our business grew, we mistakenly believed our financial situation would quickly improve. However, as our growth increased, so too did our accounts receivable and accounts payable. We became significantly behind with all of our suppliers and constantly struggled to meet payroll. LaBahn's Landscaping became embedded in debt. So many of our company checks bounced that the bank threatened to cancel our account. When another company check bounced, the bank gave us until 1:00 p.m. that day to bring in the money. I decided to hop in my car and go try to locate the mailman, who did not usually deliver the mail to our place until 4:00 p.m., much too late to satisfy the bank's demands. So off I went to find the mailman. When I found him, I explained my urgent situation and excitedly told him, "We need to get in the back of your vehicle right away and find that check!"

"Mike, you can't do that," he replied. "It's against Post Office policy." "I know I can't," I replied, "but you can. So let's go!" We then hopped into the back of his vehicle and sure enough we found that check, and I made it to the bank by the 1:00 p.m. deadline!

OUR EARLY GIVING JOURNEY

It was in the midst of this incredible financial stress that I came up with a financial goal that has paved the way for our giving journey. We were sitting in a taco shop eating carne asada and rolled tacos, trying to figure out what we were going to do with the chaos of our finances, when I took up a paper napkin. On that napkin I wrote down a single sentence that would change the course of our lives: "We are going to give away one million dollars—above our tithe—into the Kingdom of God." Of course, at the time that statement seemed absurd. Julie asked, "And how in the heck do you think we are going to do that? We can't even afford to buy a starter for our truck!"

There was no practical reason to believe that a young married couple, who had more expenses than profits, would even be able to stay in business, much less give away such an outlandish amount of money. We had no idea how we would do it; the funds were simply nonexistent. The vision seemed as flimsy as the paper napkin it was written on. We knew we had to get out of debt and put our finances in order if we were to ever give away a thousand dollars, let alone a million.

I started listening to motivational tapes, including Zig Ziglar's "See You at the Top." Ziglar's basic theme was "Ordinary people can do extraordinary things." If I was in my car I was listening to motivational tapes from Zig Ziglar, John Maxwell, or some other speaker. By hearing what the Bible said about our lives, something grew in me. This was the first time I began to believe I could create greatness and that man was designed by God to achieve meaningful things.

MINISTERING TO SINGLE MOMS

We began to help others and give in small ways, and as we did, God increased our capacity to give. We stood in the gap for the single moms who came into our lives, buying gas for those who needed it, giving them lunch money for their children, and taking kids who had no father to soccer games. The giving was more than just financial help; we knew they valued our time as much as our money.

This ministry to single moms was a real sensitive area to us because of our own backgrounds, both being raised by single parents.

"At the time we determined to set our goals to help others and give away money," Julie remembers. "We were so broke we could not even buy that stupid starter. Imagine, here we were, people without money... trying to give away money! We were just two average, ordinary people."

That is the amazing power in our story: where God shows up. What we began to accomplish had little to do with us except obedience. It was not like we made a detailed plan. It was birthed through an idea, and even that million dollar idea was put on hold right after our rolled taco dinner. We did know that to achieve something so significant as giving away a million dollars we had to first get out of debt. Towards that end, learning about money became my driving force in life, shifting from a "What do we do?" mentality to one that declared, "I need to learn all I can about financial matters."

CRAWLING AND CLAWING OUT OF DEBT

I started browsing around bookstores, looking for authors who had written books on managing and budgeting money, and how to get out of debt. The first book I read was called *Money Matters: Total Financial Control God's Way* by Larry Burkett. After reading the Burkett book, I started buying every book I could locate on the subject of money, finances, budgeting, etc. I read books by Ron Blue, Dave Ramsey, and a multitude of other Christian writers, developing an accumulated body of knowledge on money. The more I began to understand the biblical principles concerning finances, the deeper my commitment grew to run our business without any debt whatsoever.

After we made the decision to get out of debt, I made a color-coded chart listing every vendor to whom we owed any money. We voluntarily put LaBahn Landscaping on a cash basis with our suppliers and also made a schedule with them to methodically pay down our debt. Companies were willing to let us pay down our debt and pay cash for all new supplies. When we couldn't keep our agreement, I called them before they called us and said to them, "Hey, we are going to be late this month," and they always appreciated the phone call.

In the color-coded chart, each time I made a payment I would put it down on the chart. I liked to see the tangible progress on a piece of paper, with the amount we owed at the top, and then a space for the amount of the payment that particular month. We were firmly committed on this journey of working our way out of debt. Any unbudgeted money that came in went into paying off the debt. One time we made $7,000 in profit on a huge and unexpected job, and we used that check to pay off one vendor's debt. We did not buy as much as a

Slurpee out of that check.

God knows what you are going to do before you do it. I believe that's why He gives us extra money, and I'm afraid that's why sometimes He doesn't. When God knows that we have learned the lesson He is trying to teach us, and are working our way out of it, He will come into our situation... often in a way that is totally unexpected. In the case of the $7,000 check we proved faithful.

THE LANDSCAPE STARTS TO CHANGE

If LaBahn Landscaping was to significantly grow, it became apparent that we would need to look at slowly transitioning from residential to commercial properties, from mowing lawns to maintaining building complexes. One day while out canvassing for jobs, I met a man who told me, "The president of our homeowner's association is my landlord. I'll give you his phone number." I followed up on the lead, and after our meeting, the landlord decided to give LaBahn Landscaping a try.

Bonita Grande was a condo complex that sat on twenty-two acres; you could not see it from one end to the other. We were not sure how our then tiny company of just three employees could ever handle this huge account. I did not sleep very well for several nights after we reached the Bonita Grande agreement. But a large part of my story as a businessman is I learned that to accomplish anything significant it requires a willingness to get used to being uncomfortable.

About this time I realized that I didn't know much about landscaping, so I decided to go to school at Cuyamaca College and take some landscaping classes.

With Bonita Grande, we were shifting into something more professional, and we hired two more people.

Julie's role was changing from popping clutches and unloading branches to doing payroll and managing the books.

Once we secured Bonita Grande, it did not take long before we secured other condominium contracts. Our sophisticated marketing program consisted of knocking on office doors and trying to find the point of contact. We bought a riding John Deere lawnmower, hired a couple of guys, and kept taking classes and learning about landscaping. Then I realized I needed to improve my writing since I was doing proposals and other reports, so I also took some writing courses. If you do a little bit each day over a long period of time, you can accomplish a lot.

EYE PATCH SALESMAN

It was during this commercial growth in LaBahn Landscaping that the worst and the best thing happened. While I was repairing a sprinkler head, I seriously injured my eye and detached my retina. I was bedridden for two weeks with nothing to occupy me. I was young, determined, and bored out of my mind. With a patch over my eye, and a less-than-discrete hospital robe, I snuck out of my hospital room in search of the man in charge of the landscaping at Kaiser Hospital. I walked into Tom Fennel's office looking absolutely ridiculous. Imagine a man in a hospital robe, and with an eye patch, suddenly appearing in the office of a key executive at Kaiser Hospital. "Hello, my name is Mike LaBahn, and I would like to submit a proposal for the landscaping of this hospital."

A few years after that creative marketing attempt, LaBahn Landscaping was being seriously considered to be the contracting company to maintain Kaiser's facilities, and ultimately we were awarded the job. We could hardly believe what was happening to us.

It had not been that long ago that we were driving all over town picking up checks from people who owed us money just to pay our bills and avoid bounced checks. Thirty days before the Kaiser contract began, we drove together up to Pasadena, California to finalize our agreement with them.

LaBahn Landscaping was in the process of transformation. We were beginning to see the blessing of God on our business as we faithfully committed our profits to Him. We were fully committed to not only building our kingdom but His Kingdom. The pattern we were following was to be willing to be uncomfortable and to be willing to think bigger than we normally think.

STEP BY STEP GIVING

A giving ministry does not happen all at once by writing a huge check. If a person has not been giving as a faithful offering unto the Lord when they have a little money, they are not likely to start giving a large amount if they come into money through an inheritance or some other form of windfall. It has been my experience and observation that having more money makes you more of what you already are. If you have a generous heart, having more money will make you more generous but, the opposite is true too. Our ministry of giving developed over the years...bit by bit.

INTENSIFIED GIVING STARTS IN OREGON

When the concept of the million dollar pledge to God first came to us in that taco shop, we did not have a plan. We already had experienced numerous opportunities to give for smaller projects with other ministries, but we believed (and still do) that the local church is the spiritual warehouse where the majority of our giving should go (as long as that church is not stagnant and is doing something spiritually significant within the local community).

The first significant gift that can be attributed to the start of fulfilling our commitment was to Pastor Gary Clark's church in Eugene, Oregon. It might seem like this first gift was the result of a powerful supernatural moment or a sudden prompting of the Holy Spirit, but it was not. I don't think we were ever consciously thinking or discussing that this first gift was the start of fulfilling our million dollar pledge. Pastor Gary had simply challenged our congregation to consider an offering on a sacrificial scale. He called it a "first fruits" offering which had to be sacrificial: something that was not convenient, something that required a sacrifice so large that we really needed to trust God to be able to give. Proverbs 3:9-10 NIV, declares a specific promise from God - that bringing a first fruits offering to Him will bring overflowing blessings back to you.

Honor the Lord with your wealth, with the firstfruits of all your crops; then your barns will be filled to overflowing, and your vats will brim over with new wine.

God's promise was that as the first fruits offering was given, He would bless the giver. It was the faithfulness of obedience that ensured His blessing, not the size of the offering itself. For us, this opportunity to obey and give a first fruits offering as part of our million dollar pledge came at a very inopportune time. We had recently moved to Oregon and were trying to fund the building of a house, along with all the other normal monthly expenses. Our yard was cluttered with lumber, bricks, and piles of other building materials. Plus, the famous Oregon rains complicated the building project at every stage, causing costly delays due to the large, messy mud puddles around the home construction site. This was not the time to take on a costly pledge! Perhaps that is why our pastor reminded our congregation that "The opportunity to give in a significant way to God's Kingdom may come when you are planning to do something significant for yourself."

While building our home, we also decided to trust God and give sacrificially $50,000 into His Kingdom as a first fruits offering. We were rapidly learning that doing large things for God always requires faith, a willingness to make a deep commitment, and taking a sacrificial step. At that time, it was the largest check we had ever given into the Kingdom of God by far!

About one year after the first fruits offering, our church was again raising money for a very worthwhile purpose. This time, the word "sacrificial" rang heavy in our ears, and we stepped up our faith and gave the next amount towards our million dollar pledge $100,000 - twice as much as we gave in the first gift. Once we started giving, it did not stop.

The next year we decided to worship at a church nearer to our home in Cottage Grove, Oregon, so we started attending a local church called the Riverside Community Church of God. The church was going to build a family center, and we made the decision to give ten percent of the overall cost of that family center, regardless of how big the final sum became. Now that was a huge step of faith! We ended up giving a whopping $50,000.

SAN DIEGO COMPLICATIONS AND CHALLENGES

A few years later, we decided it was time to move our family back to San Diego, California, where LaBahn Landscaping's home base of operation was located, and where our children had many of their early roots and long-time friends. We bought our home in La

Mesa at the very peak of that real estate boom, and just months later, California experienced a huge real estate crash. The value of our newly purchased home dropped dramatically.

Of course, at this inopportune time, Foothills Christian Church was in the process of a building campaign to build a new, larger sanctuary. This turned out to be our most sacrificial and challenging time of giving. At a dinner with the congregation to learn more details about the expansion program, we were all asked to make a 3 year pledge. "Not equal giving, but equal sacrifice." This time, we pledged $100,000, which was to be paid over a 3 year time period. Honestly, we truly had no idea where the money to fulfill that pledge was going to come from. Looking back on those first several pledges, it was obvious that there was a clear pattern to our giving. It took faith, regardless of what the current circumstances were. *"Whoever watches the wind will not plant; whoever looks at the clouds will not reap."* (Ecclesiastes 11:4, NIV)

About that same time, Southern California caught fire – literally. We had a significant drought, and the brush all over southern California was so dry it would snap and crack underneath your feet. One of our larger clients recognized their exposure to fires, and so they hired us to remove the extensive brush surrounding all of their properties. On this one extra job we made close to $50,000. Shortly after that brush-clearing job was completed, one of our client's landscaping caught on fire. That particular job paid $50,000. When that check came in, it went straight to pay off our pledge to the church building campaign. We had completed a 3 year pledge of $100,000 in 6 months! God has a way of coming through when we have the faith to trust Him. It is well to mention that we normally only made a couple thousand dollars on any extra job. Julie and I cannot possibly view these two extra jobs as a coincidence.

A year after that campaign was paid off, Foothills expanded once again due to a severe lack of classroom space for their various teaching and ministry programs. Since this was a 1 year campaign, as opposed to the previous 3 year campaign, I assumed we would give one-third of what we gave the last time. However, when I proposed that idea to my dear wife, who seems to have a great deal more faith regarding these matters than I do, she asked me: "Mike! What are you thinking? God has always been faithful as we make our pledges."

God has a sense of humor. When I told Julie, "Okay, let's pledge 10% of whatever the church raises," I was trying to save money and manipulate the system. I honestly never dreamed that the church, so close to the last fundraiser, would ever raise $1,600,000! So, we ended up pledging $160,000. As it turns out, this was the donation that completed our goal to give $1,000,000 into the Kingdom of God.

A PROVEN SPIRITUAL PRINCIPLE

Once we formed a mindset to become givers into God's Kingdom, the financial resources for that pledge always opened up. The more we gave, the more God blessed us. On the day we finally decided to add up our giving to see how close we were to fulfilling our pledge, we learned for the first time that we had met and exceeded it. The amounts of money we planted into the Kingdom were never determined because we were trying to hit a goal...we ended up hitting that $1,000,000 pledge incidentally. Isn't that just like our God?

ORDINARY PEOPLE, EXTRAORDINARY GOD

There have been many big bumps on the rocky road of our giving journey. The entire time we have traveled on this adventure, God has always been faithful to pave His way over those pesky bumps. Yes, we have experienced serious seasons of financial drought where we could not imagine a scenario where God could come through, but we always trusted that somehow, someway, He would. At times we wondered if we would ever achieve the seemingly impossible financial goal that God put on my heart. Unexpected obstacles and suddenly-appearing potholes proliferated on the pavement on our giving highway. Even while these financial bumps and personal setbacks kept jarring and tossing us from side to side, we slowly made persistent (though sometimes agonizingly slow) progress towards our giving goal. Literally in spite of ourselves, and even with some very poor financial decisions, God proved faithful to us time and time again, honoring our hearts and our intentions to bless His Kingdom.

Remember, God's financial plan for your life will not always add up and make accounting sense on paper, but it will always work. He always comes through with the provision you will need to fulfill His plan for His purposes.

DON'T LOOK AT CIRCUMSTANCES

We determined to give away money during all seasons, even during the huge recession, regardless of how much or how little income was coming into our business at the time.

Sow your seed in the morning, and at evening let your hands not be idle, for you do not know which will succeed, whether this or that, or whether both will do equally well. Ecclesiastes 11:6, NIV

As we gave, God steadily provided. Here's the simple spiritual reality, God can take anyone and do great things with his/her life.

When they saw the courage of Peter and John and realized that they were unschooled, ordinary men, they were astonished and they took note that these men had been with Jesus. Acts 4:13, NIV

He does not require any spectacular giftedness or extreme talents. God can use *"unschooled, ordinary men."* If God only used the gifted and the talented, then He would have overlooked us and moved on to another couple far more qualified to fulfill His plan. We are the epitome of a normal, ordinary couple, complete with our faults and failings.

GOD GIVES VISION

God puts a vision into the hearts of men. Men then decide how to respond to that vision. Those who possess a desire to cooperate with Him will start to obey the challenge, counting on God to provide the provision. God takes ordinary people with a willingness to serve Him and does extraordinary things through them. If God can take two people like us, with our broken beginnings and very limited means, and use us to give away one million dollars, what can He do with you?

In truth, we never experienced a powerful, supernatural vision from the heavens that led us to declare, "God has given us divine instructions to do this." No deep voice came roaring out of the heavens, leading us every step of the way on our giving journey. No cumulous cloud suddenly appeared over our front porch in El Cajon with a dollar sign in the middle. None of that happened. Instead, we were and are just two God-fearing, God-loving people who read His Word and applied it to the fire of daily living. In that process, we learned some valuable lessons on how God can use us if we just open up our hearts and our pocketbooks for His

Kingdom.

Bill Wilson, the founder of Metro World Child in New York, which now ministers to 100,000+ kids each week, essentially said, "I never had a call on my life, never heard a call, and never needed a call. The need was the call." The need was our call as well.

ORDINARY PEOPLE, EXTRAORDINARY NEW GOALS

Our next goal is to tell our story. We are planning to raise ten million dollars for the Kingdom of God, while we are still living, and to encourage other businesspeople and individuals to join us in collectively giving one hundred million dollars into the Kingdom. We hope to challenge and inspire both businessmen and individuals, young and old, to have the faith to give into the Kingdom of God. He is the God of limitless resources. The only limit comes from us and what we tell ourselves we cannot do. Our prayers, requests, and thoughts are often too small. Our expectations are too low.

When was the last time you did something for the first time? When was the last time you attempted to do something that you could not do without God? We are not supposed to be in the harbor tied to the dock. He wants us to be free, sailing the waters of freedom, blessing and giving generously to others.

Chapter 1

WHAT IS BIBLICAL GIVING?

Would you give your all to
help someone out? Why or
why not?

Would you give to
someone who cannot
repay?

What do you do when
giving involves more than
donating money?

What other sorts of things
have you given?

How are you at continuing
to give? Do you run out
of steam, or do you keep
giving until the needy are
satisfied?

Everything in God's creation was made to give continuously.

The first verse many Christians memorize is John 3:16, NKJV: *For God so loved the world that He gave His only begotten Son, that whosoever believes in Him should not perish but have everlasting life.* The very foundation of the Christian faith is a gift. Because of His love for the world, God gave not time or money but His only Son. And this Son, Jesus Christ, in turn, willingly gave up His life as a sacrifice for the atonement of sins.

As Christians, we are to imitate our Namesake. Even a casual glance at the Gospels shows that in the years before His death, Jesus was preoccupied with serving and giving to others: *Just as the Son of Man did not come to be served, but to serve, and to give His life a ransom for many* Matthew 20:28. This is how we too are to live.

For this reason, my wife Julie and I long ago established service and giving as primary goals. We want to do the best we can to better the lives of people we come into contact with. The apostle Paul's principle outlined in 2 Corinthians 8:14 has been foundational in our marriage: *At this present time your abundance being a supply for their need, so that their abundance also may become a supply for your need, that there may be equality.* Much of our time is spent ministering to what former president Jimmy Carter once called "the forgotten people of our society."[1] One such woman who has touched our lives in a profound way is our friend Susie.

Susie was thirty-three when she and her five-year-old daughter Debbie literally rolled into our lives after a terrible automobile accident. The van they had been riding in had rolled over, giving them various bruises but no serious injuries – at least, no serious physical injuries. But they were emotionally wounded. As we got to know Susie, we learned she had been brought up by religious but emotionally distant parents and had married a man who, rather than loving and leading his family like the Bible calls a husband to do, had mistreated Susie and Debbie in every way you can imagine. Shortly after we met them, Susie's abusive, drug-addicted, chronically unemployed husband abandoned them.

By the time she crashed into our lives, just about everything possible was going wrong for Susie. Like many abandoned wives, she had no specific trade or professional training. She and her daughter had needs on every level: emotional, physical, spiritual, and of course financial. They were so deeply wounded that most people avoided them. To be perfectly honest, they would not have been welcome in many American churches today. They required much love, acceptance, time, work, counsel, encouragement, and, for a time, regular financial assistance.

For this reason, the first five years of our relationship with Susie and Debbie were one-sided: we gave and they took. We provided childcare five days a week for Debbie while Susie went to work. This may seem like no big deal, but at the time we did not have children of our own, and our service to Susie and her

1 - Jimmy Carter Quotes. (2012) Retrieved from
http://www.ascensiongateway.com/quotes/jimmy-carter/index.htm

daughter was a tremendous commitment and sacrifice of our time and resources. Susie would drop Debbie off at our house early in the morning and then go to work. Julie would take Debbie to school and pick her up when school let out. During these five years, we began to have children of our own. To take Debbie to school or collect her afterwards, Julie would have to wake a baby in the morning or in the middle of a nap in the afternoon. With sleepy, fussy infants, our house was in constant turmoil.

As our young daughters grew from babies to little girls, it became more challenging to have Debbie at our home. She was selfish, temperamental, careless, and increasingly difficult to discipline. Therapists are fond of saying, "Hurting people hurt people," and through no fault of her own, this was certainly true in young Debbie's case. Although we made allowances for her because we knew she had not known much loving care or discipline before meeting us, Debbie became harder and harder to handle.

Her mother, meanwhile, also needed much counsel, loving, training, and encouragement. In the early years, Julie spent many hours simply loving Susie and listening to her, but God soon led us to provide help in a number of very practical ways. We accepted Susie and Debbie as family members, spending time together, helping Susie financially with groceries and job-related expenses, going to Debbie's soccer games, and providing solutions to Susie's frequent car troubles. The people of our small church painted their apartment and took up a collection to purchase a reliable car for them.

There was no way that Susie could repay us, nor did we expect her to. We did not have an abundance of time or money in those days, but we did have an abundance of love. As it always does, our money and time followed our hearts (Matthew 6:21; Luke 12:34), proving to Susie that we loved her more clearly than mere words ever could.

Things began to change about five years into
this relationship. Susie finally had a decent job— the pay
was not great but was sufficient to support herself and
Debbie—and the church we all attended had done its
duty in welcoming and nurturing them. For the first time
in many years, Susie had a sense of hope for the future.
She was maturing in her relationship with the Lord, and,
while she still needed help in many practical areas, she
was becoming whole again.

As she grew in faith and became steadier on
her own feet, Susie also began to give back in ways she
could not have done before, living out the second half
of 2 Corinthians 8:14 ...*that their abundance also may
become a supply for your need.* By this time Julie and
I had four children, and Susie decided she would have
them spend the weekend at her home once a month.
Life had not suddenly become easy for her—she was still
parenting alone and working full time. But I remember
her telling Julie, "You and Mike have done so much for
me; I want to do something for you." We were thrilled.
Over the years, we lost track of how many second
honeymoons we had because of Susie's gift to us!

As Susie became less dependent on us and
increasingly dependent on Jesus, Julie and I began
to think she might be ready to be married again.
Unfortunately, there were few godly and mature single
men in any of our circles, so we did not hold out much
hope. But God did indeed give Susie such a man, a
wonderful Christian man named George. After an
extensive courtship George asked Susie to marry him,
and as she had done so often in the past, Susie came to
Julie and I for advice. I will never forget what she said as
we talked about whether she was ready to take on a role
that had caused her so much pain in the past: "Because
I've seen you two work through the difficult roads of

marriage, and because of all the love you've poured into me, I know I can do it. I know this time I'll have the emotional capacity to succeed as a wife."

The last part of this story is the best, because it completes 2 Corinthians 8:14 *...that there may be equality.* Susie came to us as a broken person, but she left as a whole person. We became peers the afternoon I walked her down the aisle and presented her to George to become his wife.

George and Susie became wonderful servants in their church. George drove the church bus for a city-wide children's ministry, and together they led a home group and discipled and counseled others. They had a heart for people struggling to turn their lives around, so they later bought property in a rural area and started a drug rehabilitation ranch. In operation for many years now, the ranch has helped to restore countless people's lives. The Lord led Julie and me to participate behind the scenes in George and Susie's ministries, and in this way we have been blessed to indirectly touch every life they have touched.

Susie's story is an example of the difference that can be made when we determine to follow Christ's example of giving our time, our resources, and our treasure. Julie and I gave to help a woman we thought could never repay us, but we were wrong. We have been more than paid back in love and friendship. We thank God for this rich blessing.

A friend of mine has been known to say, "If we piddle away the little, we'll muddle in the puddle. But if we give God our best, we'll be blessed in the rest!" My goal for this book is to lay out for you the pattern of giving designed by God in the Bible, propose how you can respond to the command to give, discuss problems that may arise when you begin to grow in giving, and then inspire you with God's promises to live a life characterized by generous giving. As you read, understand, and practice the principles found here, you will be well on your way to growing as a godly giver.

THE CALL TO GIVE

Christians are called to be followers and imitators of Christ, which involves learning particular lessons as we grow to be more like Him. Perhaps the most often neglected area of growth for Christians is giving. Too many of us hardly even know what the word means, but it appears in some version or another over 2,000 times in the Bible (KJV)—more than the words *believing*, *prayer*, and *love* combined. So at the beginning of our journey together, let us make sure we understand what *giving* means.

Greek scholar Spiros Zodhiates defines the New Testament word for giving (*didomi*) as, "To give of one's accord...spoken of sacrifice, homage...To put in the hands, power, or possession of anyone; to give oneself; yield; surrender; to deliver oneself, meaning to consecrate or devote oneself."[2] In the Greek, this word is all-inclusive. It is personal, ongoing, and implies a continuous action.

Everything in God's creation was made to give continuously. The sun gives light, the rain gives renewal and life, the earth gives food, and trees give oxygen and nutrition. When you pick an orange fresh from the tree and cut it open you find orange seeds that, if properly cultivated, will produce more oranges. If the fruit did not produce seeds in order to give more oranges, the tree's God-created purpose would be defeated. The same goes for the sun, rain, and the earth. What would happen if any of these stopped giving? Global death would occur!

Like the giving elements that surround us in nature, we were also created with a specific giving purpose: to give glory to God. To the Christ-follower this

---

2 - Zodhiates, S. (1992). Complete Word Study Dictionary: New Testament (3rd ed.). Chattanooga, TN: AMG.

means reproducing the seeds of love and life He plants in us. This is what we do when we give of our time, talents, and treasure to God and His work through the local church. Like the orange tree, if we fail to give, we defeat our created purpose. Furthermore, we dishonor and disrespect God.

For the Christian, giving is neither an option nor a one-time obligation that we can fulfill and then move on with our busy lives. It is an imperative, progressive, ongoing, continuous command, and it does not include only the wealthiest Christians or those with the most time to volunteer for service. Every Christian is to be continually, consistently giving.

THE CONTENT OF OUR GIVING

Imagine the President of the United States chose to visit your home for dinner. Would you make advance preparations for a fine meal or would you just clear a space on the kitchen counter and call for a pizza delivery? Would you set out paper plates and plastic silverware and serve last week's cold meatloaf or would you polish your grandmother's fine china and design a menu that reflected the very best your household had to offer? These silly questions illustrate an important point: we do not serve leftovers to those we want to honor. We give them our best.

While we would certainly be right in wanting to honor the President, how much more should we want to honor God? How much more does He deserve to get our best? Yet according to a somewhat recent poll, a great majority of Christians—nearly 92%—give below what God intends.[3] It is as if Jesus came to our house and we gave Him spiritual leftovers. Trust me, the Creator of the universe is not impressed with our leftovers. But God does love it when we follow His example of generous, continual giving. We know this because of His pattern of

3 - Draper, E. (2011). "Majority of Evangelical Leaders Say Tithing Not Required." Denver Post, 4/6/11. Retrieved from http://www.denverpost.com/breakingnews/ci_17784132?

rewarding and abundantly blessing those who obediently give. So what exactly are we expected to give to God?

OURSELVES

Giving begins with us acknowledging the lordship of Jesus Christ, our need for His power and guidance in our lives, and our faith in His ability to make a difference in our giving. This is followed by yielding or giving ourselves to be used of Him. Paul uses the church in Macedonia as an example of believers who were exceptional givers because they first gave themselves:

Now, brethren, we wish to make known to you the grace of God which has been given in the churches of Macedonia, that in a great ordeal of affliction their abundance of joy and their deep poverty overflowed in the wealth of their liberality. For I testify that according to their ability, and beyond their ability, they gave of their own accord, begging us with much urging for the favor of participation in the support of the saints, and this, not as we had expected, but they first gave themselves to the Lord and to us by the will of God.
2 Corinthians 8:1-5

The Macedonians were used in a mighty way because they knew that the first thing we are to give God is not money, time, or our talents but ourselves. When we give ourselves to be used of God however He determines is best, other avenues of giving will naturally follow.

OUR TITHE

After giving ourselves to God, we can then learn how to follow Him – a process of spiritual maturation commonly known as discipleship. It has been said that "A man is not a disciple until God has control of his wallet."[4] The state of our finances reveals much about the state of our hearts and priorities in life. Luke wrote,

---

4 - Noble, M. (1990). *Teachings for Discipleship: Tithes and Offerings as a Paradigm.*

For where your treasure is, there will your heart be also
Luke 12:34.

If God and His work are your top priorities, you
will follow the Biblical commandment to give through
tithing. Malachi 3:10 says, *"Bring the whole tithe into
the storehouse, so that there may be food in My house,
and test Me now in this,' says the LORD of hosts, 'if I
will not open for you the windows of heaven and pour
out for you a blessing until it overflows.'"* The tenth,
or tithe, you give is to be a holy, set apart, and sacred
portion, your offering to the Lord of the first fruits of
your labor (Proverbs 3:9; Deuteronomy 26:13-14).

Tithing is a practice directed in both the Old
and New Testaments. In the Old Testament, believers
worshipped God and received His blessings by giving
a tithe of their increase to help those who did not have
the means to adequately provide for themselves, such as
widows, orphans, strangers, and the poor.

Tithes were also intended to help meet the needs
of those whose primary occupation and responsibility
was spiritual oversight, such as the Levites, the Israelite
tribe designated by God for lives of service as high
priests.

The New Testament emphasizes God's plan
to care for the needy and for spiritual leaders through
giving as well. Jesus refers to the traditional practice of
alms giving, or giving to the poor, when making a point
about true and sincere worship. The apostle Paul makes
note on more than one occasion of his gratitude for the
giving of a church or group of individuals that helped
meet his needs as he focused on bringing the Gospel to
others.

In both the Old and New Testament, believers
who failed to give were rebuked and/or harshly
punished. In Genesis 4, God gives blessing and favor to

Abel for giving the first and best of his labor to God but is displeased with Cain, who could not be troubled to give his best. Later in this book we'll see the example of Ananias and Sapphira (Acts 5) who were punished with death for not giving their best, as they knew to do.

The point of giving through tithing and the lesson of Cain, Ananias and Sapphira, and others who failed to do so is not that God needs our money or even that He wants a specific percentage of our money. Rather, we are meant to understand that all our income or "personal" wealth is truly the result of God's grace and blessings. Leviticus 27:30 reads, *Thus all the tithe of the land, of the seed of the land or of the fruit of the tree, is the Lord's; it is holy to the Lord.*

OUR TREASURE

We learn from 2 Peter 3:18 that as Christians we are to always be growing in grace and knowledge. This principle is applicable to our giving as well, because setting aside a tithe for God is the minimum, the beginning of our giving journey. There are several ways we can grow in giving: increasing the percentage we give to the Lord, being generous in freewill offerings, and giving alms (giving to provide for the needs of the poor).

If you, like many Christians, feel anxious or unsure about the idea of consistently tithing or increasing your giving beyond tithing, remember that we are urged to give ourselves to the Lord as a spiritual service of worship (Romans 12:1). Giving is a natural byproduct of worship and reflects a heart that is:

- Happy (1 Chronicles 29:9)
- Obedient (Exodus 35:21)
- Peaceful (2 Corinthians 9:7a; Acts 20:35)
- Responsive (1 Chronicles 29:3, 6)
- Sacrificial (Exodus 35:22-29)
- Willing (Exodus 25:2)

THE PURPOSE OF OUR GIVING

Why should Christians love to give? Because we love God, are daily striving to be more like Him, and we know that God is a giver by nature. Throughout scripture we see that He gives strength (Psalm 29:11), the desires of our hearts (Psalm 37:4), grace and glory (Psalm 84:11), what is good (Psalm 85:12), perseverance and encouragement (Romans 15:5), life to all things (1 Timothy 6:13), wisdom (James 1:5), and victory through Jesus (1 Corinthians 15:57).

Everything around us that is growing and prospering began with God's giving. Think of nature: what would happen if the sun stopped giving light, clouds stopped giving water, or plants stopped producing seeds? Eventually, there would be no more life on the planet. What happens in relationships when one partner stops giving his or her best to the other? Just as with nature, that relationship is headed for death in the long term.

Giving is who God is, and it is who we are when we accept Christ into our lives and God comes to abide in us. We become partakers of God's divine giving nature: *But as many as received Him, to them He gave the right to become children of God, even to those who believe in His name, who were born, not of blood nor of the will of the flesh nor of the will of man, but of God* John 1:12-13. How then can we not give?

As children of the Kingdom and partakers of God's divine nature, we must not practice sloppy loving, giving only when others deserve it, or when it is convenient for us. We must give and love because of who we are in God in spite of our own misgivings. To see the reality of sharing in the divine nature of God, just examine your current pattern of giving. It is the divine nature to give; it is the selfish nature to hoard.

GIVING IS INTENDED FOR OUR BLESSING

J. D. Rockefeller was once asked how much money would make him happy. While his reply, "Just one dollar more!" may seem humorous, Rockefeller's greed caused him to lose friends, health, happiness, and sleep. At one point, it was even feared he would not live to see his next birthday. He took inventory and made some drastic life changes, giving money to libraries, educational institutions, arts organizations, and other charitable causes. His depression lifted, his health and joy returned, and rather than being known for greed, Rockefeller began to be admired for his giving. Although he was not an evangelical Christian, generous giving released him from the miserliness that had shackled his relationships and health. As he began to give, he began to develop into a fulfilled and happy man. Imagine the personal benefits you might begin to see if you gave as sacrificially!

PROVIDES FOR NEEDS

The tithe is God's economic means to do the work of ministry, to extend the kingdom of God, and to support those who make their living by sharing the Gospel. The Old Testament teaches, *For the tithe... I have given to the Levites* Numbers 18:24. Paul makes it clear that the principle applies to New Testament believers as well:

If we sowed spiritual things in you, is it too much if we reap material things from you? 1 Corinthians 9:11

In praising the Philippian church for sacrificially giving to support his ministry, Paul reminds them that God rewards giving by meeting our needs: *And my God will supply all your needs according to His riches in glory in Christ Jesus.* Philippians 4:19

Scripture teaches that God *supplies seed to the sower and bread for food* when we give generously in tithes and offerings to the local church (2 Corinthians 9:10). But this does not imply we are to give carelessly. Christians are to be good stewards, prudent in budgeting and prayerfully determining which portion of our income is directed to daily necessities and which is for scattering seed (ministry at home and abroad).

SHATTERS GRIEF

According to God's Word, those who obey and worship the Lord through sacrificial giving are happy, blessed, and prosperous, and their resources are protected (Proverbs 11:25, 19:17, 22:9, 28:27; Luke 6:38, 14:14; Acts 20:35). Conversely, those who ignore this command may find their resources exploited, oppressed, attacked, slowly consumed, and forcibly destroyed. The prophet Haggai likens this effect to putting money into a *purse with holes* (1:6). This is the consequence of failing to return to God what is His, which Malachi calls a criminal offense: *Will a man rob God? Yet you are robbing Me! But you say, 'How have we robbed You?' In tithes and offerings. You are cursed with a curse, for you are robbing Me, the whole nation of you.* Malachi 3:8-9

There's a striking contrast between those who are blessed and those who are cursed by God: *Unless the LORD builds the house, they labor in vain who build it; unless the LORD guards the city, the watchman keeps awake in vain. It is vain for you to rise up early, to retire late, to eat the bread of painful labors; for He gives to His beloved even in his sleep.* Psalm 127:1-2. The word *vain* ("empty, meaningless, and useless"[5]) is used three times, along with *painful,* to describe the results of life, labor, and loved ones who are not prioritized, protected, or provided for by God.

---

5 - Zodhiates, S. (1992).

Those who build on the right foundation with the right priorities are blessed by God even in their sleep. Psalm 128:1-4 restates the same truth: *How blessed is everyone who fears the LORD, who walks in His ways. When you shall eat of the fruit of your hands, you will be happy and it will be well with you. Your wife shall be like a fruitful vine, within your house, your children like olive plants around your table. Behold, for thus shall the man be blessed who fears the LORD.*

GIVING KEEPS US ACCOUNTABLE TO GOD

Throughout the Bible, God uses the way people manage money as a gauge to determine their maturity and the amount of responsibility He gives them. Though we may be able to hide from others how we handle money, we are accountable to God for every penny entrusted to us. If He sees we are not faithful in using money the way His Word instructs, He will not entrust us with the true riches—areas of ministry, insights into Scripture, and a deeper, more intimate relationship with Him.

Being known intimately goes both ways. Psalm 103:7 tells us that God made known His ways to Moses, His acts to the sons of Israel. Moses knew the God behind the ways, but Israel simply saw the acts. Moses' responsible obedience deepened his relationship with God and resulted in God's revelation and intimate knowledge. The Psalmist says, *The secret of the Lord is for those who fear Him, and He will make them know His covenant* Psalm 25:14. The word *secret* here can also mean "counsel" or "intimacy" for those who honor, revere, and obey God.

Accountability works much the same way as a wise parent adding or removing responsibility from a child. Let's say you decide to allow your son to use your car, provided he is home before midnight and does not forget to fill up the gas tank. If he is faithful to your instruction, the next time he asks to use your car you will be more inclined to agree. But if he misses curfew and leaves the gas tank near empty, you might be more likely to revoke his car privileges until he proves his trustworthiness in a lesser area of responsibility. Jesus treats us much the same way. We cannot fake stewardship; we must be accountable with the resources given to us if we expect to be blessed with more.

Let me emphasize again that obedience to biblical financial management is at the core of discipleship. There is a direct relationship between our obedience to biblical financial instruction and our maturity in Christ. Our stewardship of these principles goes hand in hand with sonship. Luke 16:10-11 says, *He who is faithful in a very little thing is faithful also in much; and he who is unrighteous in a very little thing is unrighteous also in much. Therefore if you have not been faithful in the use of unrighteous wealth, who will entrust the true riches to you?* When I get to Heaven I do not want my transcripts to say that because of reckless habits and lack of accountability I did not even graduate from kindergarten in the school of spiritual growth.

Imagine meeting Jesus in heaven after your life has ended. The Bible teaches that we will all be asked to account for how we spent our lives and our resources. What would be your response if Jesus was to ask what you did with the money He allowed you to earn? Could you answer to how well you modeled sound, biblical financial management principles for your children? Would you be able to describe how you helped the poor and needy that you came in contact with? Do you think you would be able to say you were known as a person who shared money and time bountifully and managed your resources in a way that brought honor and glory to God?

Obviously, I am only speculating about the specific nature of the questions. We do not know what the day of reckoning is actually going to be like. I do know that when we get to heaven, Jesus is not going to be interested in the hymnbooks we used for Sunday worship. He will not ask to see the notes you took in the margins of your Bible, but I suspect He may have some questions about your use of money. And in order to hear the Lord say, *"Well done, good and faithful servant,"* we should prepare our answers now.

GIVING BRINGS GROWTH

We live and operate in a world where, as they say, the only certainties are death and taxes. But there is another guarantee (in addition to salvation) for believers: if you commit to learn, follow, apply, and obey biblical principles, over the long course of your life you will see a positive impact on your finances. You will have more blessing on your finances and experience more peace and joy than if you followed the world's influence and lived to satisfy your own pleasure. This takes self-discipline and commitment.

Too often, western Christians are more influenced by what the world tells them than by the Word of God. This affects all areas of money management. Is it possible for Christians to grow past the need for instant gratification and begin to think of others and of what God is doing in the world?

GIVING PROVIDES FOR THE LOCAL CHURCH

Time and again in both the Old and New Testaments we see examples of people giving to the local church. This is not to say Christians cannot support worthwhile charitable organizations and ministries apart from the church, but our first priority is to support the local assembly, which, when strong, will be in a position to help other ministries.

You may be familiar with the Old Testament principle of storehouse giving. Clearly, the teaching in Malachi calls for us to bring the whole tithe into the storehouse (3:10), but we are told to bring our offerings into the local storehouse as well. Later, in the New Testament, Paul does not encourage believers to give to needy causes on their own but to pool their money and give through their local church: *Now concerning the collection for the saints, as I directed the churches of Galatia, so do you also. On the first day of every week each one of you is to put aside and save, as he may prosper, so that no collections be made when I come.* 1 Corinthians 16:1-2

Paul considered giving a high priority, important enough to require instructions. Notice that he specifies when to take up a collection (every week), what to do with it (give it away), who should receive it (saints who needed assistance), and how to collect it (as a group gift from the local body of believers, not given directly to the saints). Another example of this is found in Acts 4:34-35: *For there was not a needy person among them, for all who were owners of land or houses would sell them and bring the proceeds of the sales and lay them at the apostles' feet; and they would be distributed to each as any had need.* Again two principles are highlighted. First, the early Church gave offerings and sold personal belongings to help others. Second, individual saints (Christians) did not give money directly to those in need. Instead, the congregation trusted the wisdom and discernment of the leaders and apostles to decide how and where to distribute the tithes and offerings.

Clearly, the Bible has a lot to say about giving and its contexts. Even those who have been previously unfamiliar with what giving is to look like in a Christian's life can see it has been laid out in great detail for us.

Yet knowing what we should do is no guarantee that we will follow through. The next chapter explores the direct impacts and benefits of giving to help motivate our hearts toward obedience in this key area of our walk with God.

Chapter 2

WHY GIVE?
THE CALL TO HONOR GOD

Why does giving please God?

How is God honored when we give?

How might growing in giving help you also grow as a Christian?

How does giving point the way to Christ?

Think of your own giving history. How does it show what you prioritize and love?

How can you better honor God with your finances?

Today you have an appointment with a man who makes Bill Gates look like a pauper.

If you had the opportunity to visit Bill Gates, founder of Microsoft Corporation and one of the richest men in the world, would you listen to what he had to say about financial management? What if he told you that if you made a few specific changes in your business affairs you would have more money than you know what to do with? Would you be interested in his advice?

I have good news for you. Today you have an appointment with a man who makes Bill Gates look like a pauper. Not only is he the richest man ever but the Bible says he is also the wisest (1 Kings 4:29-34). Your appointment is with King Solomon, whose words come down to us through the ages: *Honor the LORD from your wealth and from the first of all your produce; so your barns will be filled with plenty and your vats will overflow with new wine.* Proverbs 3:9-10.

This, friend, is the best financial advice you will ever receive, but you will be in the minority of Christians if you follow it! Few Christians ever joyfully honor God from their wealth. On the whole, Christians' giving (or lack thereof) is a sad commentary on the state of honoring the Lord.

This situation is not confined to individuals but is reflected in the church at large. According to the Barna

Group's 2008 report on the state of giving in Christian churches, the average family attending a Protestant church gives a combined total of about 2.5% of their income to the church and other charitable organizations. This number tends to decrease in proportion with a family's increased financial status. The group's report claimed, "Americans who earn less than $10,000 gave 2.3% of their income...whereas those who earn $70,000 or more gave only 1.2%...in fact, in absolute terms, the poorest Christians give away more dollars than all of the wealthiest Christians."[6] This includes giving to the church and benevolent organizations. Sylvia Ronsvalle notes, "And that fits with the increasing consumer mentality in the church" (Ronsvalle, 1999). [7] The good news is over 25% of evangelicals tithe and statitics show they live happier lives and have longer marriages, among many other benefits.

Like their members, most churches have a lot to learn about honoring the Lord. To honor God means not only to pay Him homage, value, respect, and esteem but also to glorify Him. He is the one who deserves all credit and fame, and we should offer Him our finances in a spirit of humble gratitude. Is it because of your wisdom, tremendous talent, and expertise that the Lord has blessed you? No! God has granted you success and favor. Understand that you have been blessed so that you might honor Him. Why does the Bible so emphasize that we are to honor the Lord with our finances?

TO DEMONSTRATE OUR LOVE

But whoever has the world's goods, and sees his brother in need and closes his heart against him, how does the love of God abide in him? 1 John 3:17

I heard a story of a pastor who was preparing a sermon one Saturday when he received a phone call from

---

6 - Moll, R. (2008). "Scrooge Lives!" Christianity Today. Retrieved from www. christianitytoday.com/ct/2008/december/10.24.html?start=2
7 - Ronsvalle, S. (1999). "The State of Church Giving through 1999." New York: Empty Tomb LLC.

his distressed neighbor. The neighbor said he needed help immediately because severe winds and rains were threatening to topple a huge tree in his front yard onto the roof of his house. The pastor explained he was not dressed for that sort of thing and was working on his Sunday sermon. The neighbor cried, "I don't care what you're doing! I need help now!"

The pastor ran out to help, destroying his new shoes in the mud, losing preparation time, and eventually returning home a soggy mess, but his generosity sowed a seed of friendship. As a result of the pastor's words and actions, the neighbor eventually came to the Lord.

An old Christian truism says, "Preach the gospel; use words if necessary." Although we may not all be pastors, we all preach sermons every day —not with words but with our actions. When you think about it logically, the act of giving is the manifestation of love. When we love someone, we give our best. What if your child developed a fatal disease and you were told that the cure was so expensive it required you to increase your income by ten percent, lower your expenses by ten percent, or both? Would you just sit by and let your child die?

Although we may talk a lot about loving others, the real test of love is what we do when real assistance is needed. If we can see a need in someone's life and withhold help even though we have the means to fulfill that need, we show signs of a closed heart. When we are thoughtful, considerate, and caring in ways that cause us to reach out and give, others feel loved and cherished. That is why words of encouragement, gifts, celebrations, remembered anniversaries, birthdays, and time spent with others, and the like are so important to people. Giving is love in action.

As we move in the realm of God's Kingdom,

this is especially true. Neither believers nor unbelievers will care what we know until they know that we care. Nowhere is this more evident than in giving our time, talents, and treasures. But others' crises rarely fit neatly into our schedules. They are inconvenient, interruptive, and involved. They sap our energy, money, and emotions. Nothing forces us to trust God more than sacrificial giving.

Giving is one of the few areas of the Christian walk that cannot be faked. Think about the various Christian disciplines: Bible study, prayer, service, worship, and giving. These disciplines communicate how we feel about God. We can and should do all these things, but in our stingy giving—our dishonoring behavior to God—we show the weakness of our love for Him.

In John 14:15, Jesus said, *If you love Me, you will keep My commandments.* In Matthew 22:37, He said, *You shall love the LORD your God with all your heart, and with all your soul, and with all your mind.* Nothing offers so practical a test of our love for Christ and others as our attitude toward money and possessions, nor does anything so test our claim to be delivered from the love of money. It seems obvious if we are not doing what His Word says about honoring the Lord through giving, that perhaps we do not really love Him.

I mentioned the following thought in the first chapter, but it bears repeating. I have a funny feeling that when we get to heaven Jesus will not ask to see our Bibles. He will not be concerned with how many verses we have highlighted. He will not be overly consumed with how many verses we have memorized. He will not ask how many committees we served on. He will not ask to see our prayer journals. I suspect He will be more concerned with how we have spent the resources, talents, and treasures He blessed us with. The record of our spending will tell Him—and us—just how much we loved and lived for Him during our time on Earth.

The simple truth is that we cannot give consistently to others until we are in love with Jesus. Out of our love for God, we love each other. We give to what we love. When we are filled with love for God, giving to His work presents no obstacle. Our giving becomes a continual cycle. Just as the earth, sun, and clouds sustain life when they continue to give according to God's order and design, so does the cycle of giving. As we who love Jesus are constantly refreshed by the Holy Spirit flowing through us, our hearts delight in giving refreshment to others. Completing the cycle, our giving flows heavenward and delights the heart of God.

OUR UNDERSTANDING OF GOD'S POWER AND PROVISION

In Deuteronomy 8:18, Moses records a set of final instructions given to the children of Israel as they prepared to enter the Promised Land after years of wandering in the wilderness. Included is this command: *But you shall remember the LORD your God, for it is He who is giving you power to make wealth, that He may confirm His covenant which He swore to your fathers, as it is this day.*

Giving of our wealth to the Lord shows that we understand who provides for us. If you think about it, we really are not giving Him anything; we are simply returning what already belongs to Him. Psalm 24:1 says, *The earth is the LORD's, and all it contains, the world, and those who dwell in it.* We understand God's ownership at a cognitive level, perhaps, but until we act on what we know, we have not truly learned the lesson. When we honor God with the first of what we produce, we acknowledge that He is the very reason we are productive and able to earn money.

Our self-reliant, "I don't need anybody but me" culture glorifies the idea of the self-made individual, but in reality there is no such thing. Did you make the air, soil, or minerals that are vital to life and sustenance? Do you control the passage of time? Is it in your power to extend your life by even one more breath? Friend, you would not even be able to walk if it were not for the life-sustaining power and protection of the Lord. He is the one who equips us, who gives us the creativity to produce anything of worth. This is a difficult concept to come to grips with, but when we truly understand and appreciate it, we will respond with hearts that want to give back for all that we have been given.

BETTER MANAGE OUR FINANCES

Does God want you to have a better marriage? Would He like your parenting skills to line up with His Word? Would He be pleased if your prayer life improved? We probably agree that the answer to these questions is yes. Then why is it so difficult to understand that the Lord would like your financial situation to improve as well? Am I saying the Lord wants to turn everybody into a millionaire? Definitely not! The Lord needs people at all income levels. But as you learn to conduct your life according to His Word, life will improve, including your finances.

Proverbs 3:6 promises, *In all your ways acknowledge Him, and He will make your paths straight.* The word acknowledge has a rich meaning: "knowing, being aware of, and having fellowship with. You cannot have fellowship with God if you do not acknowledge His involvement in your life. It is difficult for God to straighten out your finances if you are withholding them from Him.

Maybe you feel you cannot honor the Lord

with the first of your produce because you have not acknowledged Him in your management of the resources He has let you produce. In the financial seminars I conduct, only about 5% of the people attending have wills or a budget, and most Christians I talk to save virtually nothing for the future, including money for their next set of tires. If we acknowledged God in our finances and managed our money the way His Word calls for, we would have more money. Pastor Gary Clark of Eugene Christian Fellowship is fond of saying, "If you learn everything the Bible says about money and are obedient to God's principles, over the long course of your life you will have more money than if you continue to manage your finances according to your own or the world's ideas."

The more we practice sound, biblical financial principles, the straighter our path. You see, we honor the Father not only with the first fruits of our produce but also with how we earn money, pay our bills, and follow His principles.

The principle of giving and receiving continues until we break the cycle of giving. Those who do well with what they are given will be given more so they can give more. You may think giving will make you poorer, but the opposite is true, according to the principle in Proverbs 3:9-10, NLT: *Honor the Lord with your wealth and with the best part of everything you produce. Then He will fill your barns with grain, and your vats will overflow with good wine.*

It is a great comfort to know that we serve a loving God who has our best interests at heart. God's ways work, and they work out for our good. God is not as concerned with whether we have honored Him in the past as He is with whether we will honor Him in the future. God honors those who honor Him:

Those who honor Me I will honor, and those who

despise Me will be lightly esteemed. 1 Samuel 2:30.

Honoring the Lord from your wealth will end up blessing you in return.

HELP THE WEAK

Acts 20:35 provides another reason to give: *You must help the weak.* That means that giving is also a ministry. Matthew 25:34-40 spells this out nicely for us:

Then the King will say to those on His right, "Come, you who are blessed of My Father, inherit the kingdom prepared for you from the foundation of the world. For I was hungry, and you gave Me something to eat; I was thirsty, and you gave Me something to drink; I was a stranger, and you invited Me in; naked, and you clothed Me; I was sick, and you visited Me; I was in prison, and you came to Me." Then the righteous will answer Him, "Lord, when did we see You hungry, and feed You, or thirsty, and give You something to drink? When did we see You a stranger, and invite You in, or naked, and clothe You? And when did we see You sick, or in prison, and come to You?" The King will answer and say to them, "Truly I say to you, to the extent that you did it to one of these brothers of Mine, even the least of them, you did it to Me."

These verses tell us that when we give to the weak and the poor we are giving to Christ, who is always on their side. When we involve ourselves in the lives of those who are downtrodden, we are indeed ministering unto Jesus.

This is a simple concept with a multitude of meanings. For example, helping the weak could mean a period of concentrated effort on your part to bring someone to salvation. It could also mean volunteering or giving resources to aid organizations. It could mean giving in excess of your tithe to benefit God's work at your local church or to worldwide evangelization through missions. We followers of Christ must believe—and practice—that it is truly more blessed to give than to receive. Those of us who want to give need only keep our hearts and eyes open.

TRAIN OUR HEARTS

Let's face it: ours is a consumer oriented culture in which we are daily, even hourly, tempted by materialism. Jesus understands this pressure, but He calls us to be different from our culture. In Mark, we read of Jesus' response to a wealthy young man: *Looking at him, Jesus felt a love for him, and said to him, 'One thing you lack: go and sell all you possess, and give to the poor, and you will have treasure in heaven; and come, follow Me'* Mark 10:21. Jesus told the man if he truly wanted to be a follower of Jesus, he had to go and sell everything. Does this mean we must go and sell everything to follow Jesus? No, not necessarily, but it does mean we should be willing to do so. When we give, we train our hearts not to love material things.

There is nothing wrong with material possessions, but they become idols when we spend all of our time and energy maintaining what we have or scheming to acquire more. The principle to be learned from this verse in Mark is that giving away your possessions is actually the cure for materialism, and there is an added benefit: giving can help us stay out of debt. Most of us simply do not make enough money to both have consumer debt and maintain a lifestyle of giving. Even if your income is healthy enough that you can give while in debt, consider how much more you could give if you did not have debt.

MEET NEEDS WITHIN THE BODY OF BELIEVERS

We also give in order to meet other Christians'

needs. We've already discussed how giving can help
non-believers, but Romans 12:13 also instructs us to
contribute to the needs of the saints. Every week when
I sit in church, I am surrounded by people at all income
levels, from those living in abundance to those too
burdened with making ends meet to even enjoy worship.
The trick is to get the two together. This requires
generosity on the part of the person with plenty and
humility on the part of the person with little.

Some people simply do not make enough money
to live on, but God loves to meet their needs through
those He has blessed with financial resources. For
instance, God has connected Julie and me with various
single parents over the years. One simple way God
inspired us to give: we opened an account at a local gas
station and told certain single parents we knew to go
down and fill up their tanks whenever they needed gas.
To single parents regularly short on resources—actually,
to any family who has been affected by economic
conditions such as our country has experienced
recently—this meant a lot. There are many other ways
to help Christians in need. If you have a desire to honor
God in this way, your pastor will likely have many ideas
to get you started.

POINT THE WAY TO CHRIST

*The LORD is good to all, and His mercies are
over all His works. All Your works shall give thanks
to You, O LORD, and Your godly ones shall bless You.*
Psalm 145:9-10

In Psalm 145, David blesses, praises, and exalts
God's name, works, acts, majesty, greatness, goodness,
righteousness, kingdom, and power in order to make
God's goodness known to upcoming generations.
Similarly, in the book of Joshua we learn that the
Israelite elders built monuments to commemorate God's

goodness and miraculous acts *that all the peoples of the earth may know that the hand of the LORD is mighty, so that you may fear the LORD your God forever* (Joshua 4:24). Our giving also provides a testimony for future generations. As we give tithes and love offerings by faith, our children see us trusting God, see God answering prayer, and hear stories of His wondrous deeds.

Our giving also may encourage non-believers to find faith in Christ. I once read about Edward Kimball, a nineteenth-century Sunday school teacher, who gave of his time to lead a Boston shoe clerk to faith in Jesus Christ. The clerk, Dwight L. Moody, became an evangelist and, in England in 1879, awakened evangelistic zeal in the heart of Fredrick B. Meyer, a pastor of a small church. While preaching at an American college, Meyer, in turn, led a student named J. Wilbur Chapman to Christ.

Chapman engaged in YMCA work and employed a former professional baseball player named Billy Sunday to do evangelistic work. Sunday held a revival in Charlotte, North Carolina, where a group of local men became so enthusiastic that they planned another campaign to bring Mordecai Ham to town to preach. At this revival, a young man named Billy Graham came forward to receive Christ during the song "Just as I Am." Graham yielded his life to Jesus Christ and went on to preach the gospel to millions throughout the world. This all started with Edward Kimball's small act of giving a little time and talent. Like ripples in a pond, the circles of influence from giving our time, talents, and treasure move outward in ever widening dimensions.

INCREASE OUR FAITH

"Faith promise" is a concept in which believers pray for God to supernaturally provide extra money, which in turn can be given to further missions. A friend of mine was on a limited income but wanted to try this. At first, he only prayed for $20. God provided it as a result of someone's kindness. His faith strengthened, our friend prayed to give $50 to missions. What do you suppose happened? His finances were blessed to match his faith, and he was able to give $50 to missions. Before long it was a pattern; each year that he prayed in faith to be able to give more, he was blessed to do it.

Giving stretches our faith. Scripture teaches, *Now faith is the assurance of things hoped for, the conviction of things not seen... And without faith it is impossible to please Him, for he who comes to God must believe that He is and that He is a rewarder of those who seek Him* (Hebrews 11:1, 6). We do not initially see what happens to our tithes and offerings. We have to use our faith to trust God to reward us.

Giving is evidence of God's grace at work in our hearts. The degree and nature of one's giving are generally proportional to the amount of grace one has experienced. Paul says, *Now, brethren, we wish to make known to you the grace of God which has been given in the churches of Macedonia* (2 Corinthians 8:1). This grace was the Macedonian church's willingness to give out of extreme poverty—not only according to their ability but beyond!

Chapter 3

BENEFITS OF GIVING:
THE DIVIDENDS OF GOD

How has God demonstrated His kindness and mercy to you? Think of specific examples.

What examples of positive and negative sowing and reaping have you seen in your life or in the lives of others?

Why does God give? Why do/should we give?

In which areas do you sense God calling you to improve in your daily giving to others?

Is it wrong to give because you'd like to earn eternal rewards?

God is a gracious and abundant giver, not a stingy, miserable miser.

How many financial managers can guarantee returns such as God promises in the verse below and throughout the Bible? Unlike your earthly investment portfolio, sacrificial giving to further God's kingdom is backed by His promises of provision, protection, and repayment in kind. These are guarantees no financial manager can give.

Give, and it will be given to you. They will pour into your lap a good measure—pressed down, shaken together, and running over. For by your standard of measure it will be measured to you in return. Luke 6:38

It is never a matter of *if* God's promises will be fulfilled, only when. The beauty of these dividends is that they last forever and are of far more value than any return on an earthly investment. In fact, Peter describes our inheritance as imperishable, undefiled, and kept in heaven for us (1 Peter 1:3-4). Talk about a good investment!

You have probably heard of people taken advantage of by unscrupulous investors who cheat them out of what was to be their golden-years retirement. These scam artists skip town and leave behind people with broken dreams and busted bankbooks. Investing in the bank of heaven is not like that. God always pays good returns on kingdom investments.

In Scripture, the dividend that comes from godly giving has been variously translated as fruit, reward, and profit. In *The Message: New Testament with Psalms and Proverbs,* Eugene Peterson paraphrases Philippians 4:17 as, *I do want you to experience the blessing that issues from generosity.*[8] Too many Christians feel that they just don't make enough money to be able to give even ten percent of it to God, but time and again we see that God desires to bless and prosper those who obediently, cheerfully, and generously give according to His prompting. As we take this journey of faith we are promised:

> God won't withhold good from an upright person (Psalm 84:11).
>
> Riches, honor, and life come from humility and fearing God (Proverbs 22:4).
>
> God will give us the desires of our hearts (Psalm 37:4)
>
> God will bless the works of our hands (Deuteronomy 28:2, 8, 12-13).
>
> Those who love God will be delivered, honored, answered, protected, and given long life and salvation (Psalm 91:14-16).
>
> All our needs will be met by God (Philippians 4:19)

We also know from Scripture that God is no liar; in fact, He is incapable of lying (Titus 1:2; Hebrews 6:18). So when He says He will do something, you can mark it down–He will do it. Moses wrote in Numbers 23:19, *God is not a man, that He should lie, nor a son, of man that He should repent. Has He said, and will He not do? Or has He spoken, and will He not make it good?* Throughout history, God's track record in promise keeping is 100%, so you can rest assured He means what

---

8 - Peterson, E. (1995). "The Message: New Testament with Psalms and Proverbs." Colorado Springs, CO: NavPress.

He says (1 Kings 8:56; Isaiah 55:10-11).

HE WILL PROTECT AND PROVIDE FOR YOU

He Himself has said, "I will never desert you, nor will I ever forsake you," so that we confidently say, "the Lord is my Helper, I will not be afraid. what shall man do to me?" Hebrews 13:5-6

As adopted sons and daughters of God, we have the right to ask God for His intervention and His will in our finances. When we give according to God's principles and are obedient to His instructions in all areas of life, we can and should look to Him for help. God says in Malachi 3:11, *Then I will rebuke the devourer for you, so that it will not destroy the fruits of the ground.* This verse promises that God will protect our finances. This protection can take many forms, from something as seemingly insignificant as a friend paying back a $50 loan at the moment you needed to cover the grocery bill to being spared a layoff notice at work—or even being promoted—during a down economy. God has also protected His children from the pain of unforeseen expenses like an unusually long-lived old roof or home appliance. I have personally experienced this type of protection and have talked with many people who have seen it in their lives as well.

I knew of a family in Missouri who tithed faithfully and lived according to biblical principles but, due to a labor dispute, the father was out of work. They had no income and no food to eat. One day the wife felt that she was supposed to go to the grocery store. The impression was so strong that it was almost as if a voice had audibly told her to go. There, she was led to load her shopping cart with groceries that she had no money to buy. In faith she pushed her cart to the cash register. As the groceries were being rung up, a stranger in line behind her said, "I'll pay for your groceries." Another

member of this same family found a wallet containing
six hundred dollars in cash and two signed blank
checks. They turned the wallet and all its contents over
to the police department, and three months later, the
wallet's owner sent back a letter of thanks and enclosed
three hundred dollars. Over the next ten years, every
Christmas the family received a card with one hundred
dollars from this grateful stranger. What a testimony
of God's provision for this family in response to their
obedience and desire to honor Him.

The Lord intervenes in our finances based on
what we have done in the past and what He knows
we will do in the future. If your children follow the
guidelines and principles you have set for them, are
you likely to give them more freedoms and blessings
to supplement their current level of improved
responsibility? Of course you are. So is God with us.

Isn't the reverse also true? If your children are
disobedient, are you likely to reward them or give them
more responsibilities? Of course not. Irresponsible
children not only disappoint their parents, they also
hurt themselves. In the same way, we rob God by not
giving, and we also rob ourselves. God wants to protect
and bless us, but we tie His hands by not doing what His
Word says. We need to face the facts. God wants to do
His part. He is waiting for us to do ours.

You may think that wanting God's blessing is
not the right motivation for giving. Perhaps not. But it
is not a bad place to start. God is capable of correcting
our motives to align with His, so it is better to start
obeying now than to sit and wait until we feel like giving.
Whether your reason is to gain something good from
your giving or to avoid losing God's positive intervention
in your life, find a way to make yourself available to all
that God wants you to experience. If you are not ready
to trust God with a full tithe, start with giving just one

percent of your income. But here's the kicker: your giving should grow regularly, not stagnate at the level you feel comfortable with. If you start out giving one percent, double it in three months to two percent. Once you have been faithful at two percent for awhile, increase the amount again to four or five percent. Continue this pattern until you are regularly giving God at least a tenth of your gross income.

If you are new to giving, watch out: you will quickly find that the supernatural is real in this life. God is always watching and waiting for us to show our obedience to His Word and faith in His promises. All it takes is a little faith that God will do what He has promised; in fact, the Bible teaches that even faith the size of a mustard seed (one of the smallest seeds) can accomplish much. He is waiting for you to be obedient and trust Him so that He can intervene in your finances and bring abundant blessings into your life.

Two thousand years ago, a little boy saw people in need of food and unreservedly gave all he had to help meet the need. Considering that he was just one in a crowd of well over five thousand hungry people that day, the boy's meager offering (five barley loaves and two fishes) could hardly make an impact. But the difference lies in the person to whom the boy gave. Jesus was thankful for this sacrificial gift and used it in a miraculous way to feed the entire crowd. Not only did everyone, including the boy, eat until they were satisfied, there were plenty of leftovers (John 6:1-13). Just as the boy found his needs provided for according to the miraculous riches of heaven, we also find that God provides bountifully for those who care for His kingdom. What we give will be exponentially multiplied and returned to us so that our needs are also met.

HE WILL PROSPER AND BLESS YOU

Many of the wonderful promises in the Bible are conditional promises ("if you do _____, then you can expect _____," e.g.; Exodus 19:5; Deuteronomy 11:13-15; Psalm 91:9-10; Isaiah 48:18; Matthew 21:22; Luke 17:6). One such promise involves meditating on Scripture; in Joshua 1:8 God promises, *This book of the law shall not depart from your mouth, but you shall meditate on it day and night, so that you may be careful to do according to all that is written in it; for then you will make your way prosperous, and then you will have success.* Giving is an if/then conditional promise. When God's conditions for giving have been met, blessings will follow. Paul writes in Philippians 4:19, *And my God will supply all your needs according to His riches in glory by Christ Jesus.*

As we boldly speak out the promises of God, fully convinced that God will provide financially, we position ourselves for prosperity. W. H. Murray wrote, "Until one is committed, there is hesitancy, a chance to draw back... the moment one definitely commits oneself, then providence moves too, and a whole stream of events erupt—all manner of unforeseen incidents, meetings, persons, and material assistance, which no man could have dreamed would come his way and begins to flow towards him."[9]

There's a story told about a young man who was accepted with his family to the African mission field, but he was sadly disappointed to discover his wife could not stand the climate. Heartbroken, the man returned home and prayerfully determined to use all the money he could make for the kingdom of God. His father, a dentist, had begun to make an unfermented wine to be used in communion services. The young man took over this venture and developed it until it became successful. The man's name was Welch, and as you may suspect, his venture became the world-famous grape juice enterprise.

---

9 - Murray, W.H. (1951). "The Scottish Himalayan Expedition." London: Dent & Sons, Inc.

Welch has given hundreds of thousands of dollars to the work of missions. This man's prosperity did not come easily, but he fought to be obedient to God despite many setbacks. His perseverance resulted in blessing and prosperity for God's kingdom.

I have a friend who sacrificially gave of his time, talents, and treasures even when he was poorly paid at a church in the Southwest. He would regularly find his refrigerator and wallet empty before the end of the month. On one occasion he cried out to God in faith, reminding God of His promise to supply our needs if we but obey. Shortly after this, he was invited to a dinner where he made some friends who helped him get speaking engagements that paid much-needed honorariums. Was that just my friend's lucky day? No— rather, God was following through on His promise to honor, bless, and prosper men and women with hearts set on kingdom purposes, who obediently sow into His kingdom. He shows us His generosity so that we can then become conduits of blessing to the world, ministering to the needy and the unsaved.

Scripture teaches us to pray, *Give us this day our daily bread* (Matthew 6:11). It also says, *You do not have because you do not ask* (James 4:2). One way to be a giver in God's kingdom is to pray and then expectantly watch for God to abundantly meet your needs. This is known to many as the principle of sowing and reaping, and it is found in Galatians 6:7, *Don't be deceived. God is not mocked, for whatever a man sows, that he will also reap.* The principle of sowing and reaping is simply understood: whatever you invest in the world, you will receive back. You decide what that investment will be. The principle works in every area of life. Wherever you are generous, you will receive generosity again; whenever you hoard, you will receive in kind. Or as many of us better know it, "What goes around comes around."

God is a gracious and abundant giver, not a miser. His blessings are much more than material, but those who do not look past earthly credits and debits cannot grasp this. The life of David Livingstone offers us an example of God prospering giving in the heavenly realm. Livingstone, who many believe to be one of the greatest Christian missionaries who ever lived, gave his life to labor in obscurity for Christ in Africa, thousands of miles from his homeland. When he died, his body was brought back to England and buried in Westminster Abbey. Crowds thronged the streets to pay him tribute.

At Livingstone's tomb, one man stood alone, weeping. He and Livingstone had been childhood friends, and when he'd heard about Livingstone going to Africa as a missionary the man had urged against it and called Livingstone crazy for wanting to go. As the two went their separate ways, this man pursued his own fortunes in London, lived only for himself, and became known to very few people. Livingstone, meanwhile, dedicated his life to God and serving others, and he became the best known and loved man of his day. That day at Livingstone's tomb, his former friend cried out, "I put the emphasis on the wrong world!" He finally recognized the value of Livingstone's life investment, but to his great regret it was too late to let his friend know.

You see, what we give to God and others is never misspent or wasted. God will never allow Himself to be in debt to any man but will always repay what has been given in His name. Proverbs 19:17 reminds us, *One who is gracious to a poor man lends to the Lord, and He will repay him for his good deed.* In Ephesians 3:20-21 Paul writes, *Now to Him who is able to do far more abundantly beyond all that we ask or think, according to the power that works within us, to Him be the glory in the church and in Christ Jesus to all generations forever and ever. Amen.*

God is the best and should have your best. If
this isn't enough to motivate you to give, His promise
to bless and prosper those who give means it is in your
best interest to give Him your best. Giving back to God
is a way to make your little become a lot. I believe if
two people with similar abilities and opportunities go
through life earning about the same amount of money,
over the course of their careers, the one who consistently
and obediently gives to God will have more money, less
debt, and substantially more peace and joy than the
one who never learns to give. Remember the example
of David Livingstone and his friend: if you keep your
money for yourself, you may temporarily add to your
little kingdom here on earth, but when you give to God's
kingdom, your storehouse will overflow.

Chapter 4

WHY WE DO NOT GIVE

Think about the many reasons people do not give. Which have applied to you in the past?

What did you do to overcome these obstacles?

Are you judgmental of others who do not give?

What attitude do you think Christ wants you to have about these people?

How might a better understanding of the reasons people do not give help you encourage others in giving?

"Then I will rebuke the devourer for you..."

It saddens me to think a chapter of this nature is even necessary for God's people. Giving should be the result of a fundamental understanding of our relationship with God, our way of joyfully acknowledging that God has given us everything we have. Too many Christians fail to mature in giving because they never reach that understanding and thus never fully appreciate God's provision for their lives.

I have given numerous classes, seminars, and sermons on the importance of giving. At some point in my presentation I usually say, somewhat tongue in cheek, "If you don't give consistently to God and His work, come talk to me, because I'd love to know why." As of yet, no one has been willing to be transparent enough to respond, but that does not mean that they are successfully hiding their lackluster giving record.

In 2 Corinthians 8:5 we see that the origin of all godly giving is an intimate relationship with the Lord Jesus: *And this, not as we had expected, but they first gave themselves to the Lord and to us by the will of God.* This intimacy cannot be assumed and does not just happen by chance. We must push past apathy, ignorance, unaccountability, and selfishness to get to a place of deep love and commitment to the Lord. This struggle, which is at the heart of the attitudes and perspectives discussed in this chapter, is the real reason we do not give.

WE HAVE A UFO MINDSET

One Sunday, Johnny Hunt, senior pastor of a baptist church in Woodstock, Georgia, told his congregation about a recent robbery of a church in nearby Atlanta. Two armed men had entered the church during its worship service and stolen the offering. Pastor Hunt's congregation was outraged at the crime, but he was quick to reply that many of them had more in common with the thieves than they would readily admit. He accused them of being UFOs—Uncommitted, Freeloading Onlookers—a crime that also victimizes the church and angers God. Hunt's congregants got the point—Christians who fail to give are hardly better than armed robbers.

Are you getting this? We rob God (Malachi 3:8) when we do not support the local church. Many of us have become blasé about our lack of giving. Arrested in our development, we remain uncommitted, freeloading onlookers, content to show up to church on Sunday just looking for how we can be served, how we can be helped or ministered to, and unconcerned with how the work of God will be carried out apart from our participation. Our crime against God clearly does not bother us; otherwise, wouldn't we give?

As if this crime were not enough, I believe with my whole heart that when we fail to give, we also rob ourselves. What blessings might we have received if we had been more careful to give? God has a plan for our lives, and an essential part of that plan is for us to be caring, generous, and giving Christians, receiving His abundant blessings and favor as we obey and live for Him. If we truly understood and believed this, we would change our hearts and take a deeper look at how we support the work of God.

WE THINK WE CAN FOOL GOD

A minister of the gospel was debating the importance of obedience to God's Word with a certain man. When the minister asked if the man had ever been baptized, the man replied, "No, sir, I haven't. But the dying thief was never baptized, and he went to heaven." The minister then urged the man to be more faithful in church attendance. The man replied. "Why should I? The dying thief didn't go to church, and he was saved." Finally, the minister encouraged the man to be diligent in his duty to support the local assembly with financial gifts. To that the man responded, "That's not necessary, either. The dying thief never gave one cent to missions or anything like that." Turning away with a disgusted shake of his head, the man of God said, "Mister, the only difference I can see between you and the thief on the cross is that he was a dying thief and you're a living one."

God wanted to bless this man with gifts too wonderful to imagine. But the sad truth is that because he thought he had outsmarted God, he would never know what God could have provided. When we decide not to give to God's work, we are in effect saying, "God, I know more about money than you." When we take this approach, God allows us to go our financial way alone.

Such disobedience hurts us more than it hurts God or others. God is not wanting for anything, but we certainly are. When we are not obedient in giving, we damage our relationship with God and our relationship with money. If we believe everything belongs to God and that He decides who gets what, does it not seem logical for Him to bless those who give as He directs?

This principle holds true in all areas of life. Take our relationships, for example. The Bible teaches us not to be harsh with one another. If I am harsh with my children over a long period of time, my harshness will hurt my relationship with them. Eventually they will become adults who can choose not to spend time with me. In the long run, my harshness would cost me not only my relationships with my children but with my future precious grandchildren as well.

WE ARE APATHETIC

Another reason we do not give is that we simply do not care what Jesus or Scripture says about money, giving, or obedient living. Suppose you went to church and found posters listing the names of every church member along with a detailed report of each person's personal giving over the last year. What would your reaction be? Such public exposure might embarrass or anger you. It might even cause you to leave the church.

If we would be angry or embarrassed about everyone at church knowing how much money we gave, why are we not already embarrassed that Jesus knows? Too often Christians are far more concerned with what others think than with what the Lord Jesus Christ thinks. Don't be indifferent to God's passionate call to give!

WE LIVE FINANCIALLY UNACCOUNTABLE LIVES

Whenever I begin a workshop about financial accountability, one of two things typically happens in the audience. Sometimes the room goes quiet and I can hear rustling as people shift uncomfortably in their seats. Other times, someone will speak up to object, citing the Sermon on the Mount where Jesus says:

So when you give to the poor, do not sound a trumpet before you, as the hypocrites do in the synagogues and in the streets, so that they may be honored by men. Truly I say to you, they have their reward in full. But when you give to the poor, do not let your left hand know what your right hand is doing, so that your giving will be in secret; and your Father who sees what is done in secret will reward you. Matthew 6:2-4

Well-meaning Christians generally believe they speak with a full understanding of the passage, but too often it is taken out of context. This verse applies to almsgiving (giving to the poor), not giving in general. We should definitely give alms in secret to avoid embarrassment or causing dependency in those we are helping. But being accountable to one another and having an open record of giving should not be misconstrued as showing off or sounding our own trumpets to garner acclaim or prestige.

If you are a regular attendee at a local church and you understand that Jesus knows your record of giving anyway, perhaps a less radical practice would be to meet annually with your pastor to review your W-2 form and your annual giving statement and to talk about your goals for giving and/or tithing for the next year. Your pastor may have some suggestions or have access to literature or resources to help you deal effectively with biblical financial principles. At this meeting, you could also take a look at your pastor's W-2 statement and annual giving record. Can you imagine the intimacy and trust created by full disclosure and accountability between pastor and congregation? This would create a level of transparency and an environment of love, openness, and acceptance only seen in churches that accomplish the greatest things for God's kingdom.

WE LACK PROPER LOVE FOR GOD

If all these excuses were not real problems in today's church, I would not need to address the next reason people don't give: lack of love for God. Going back to Matthew's Gospel, we see how the Pharisees baited Jesus:

One of them, a lawyer, asked Him a question, testing Him, "Teacher, which is the great commandment in the Law?" And [Jesus] said to him, "'You shall love the Lord

*your God with all your heart, and with all your soul,
and with all your mind. This is the great and foremost
commandment. The second is like it, "You shall love
your neighbor as yourself."'* Matthew 22:35-39

Friend, these are Jesus' own words. He says the
most important thing we can do is to love God with all
we are and all we have. When we love someone with our
complete being, we find out what is important to our
beloved. We make it our business to please our beloved.
We do everything within our power to preserve our
relationship with this person.

In John 14:15, Jesus says, *If you love Me,
you will keep My commandments.* It would seem the
reverse would be true as well: if you do not keep His
commandments, you do not love Him. What does this
say about the majority of American Christians who
do not give? Too often the truth is that God gets the
leftovers. How you and I spend our money truly reveals
who or what we love and worship. Our giving gives us
away. Oswald Chambers wrote, "We do not consciously
disobey God, we simply do not heed Him. God has given
us His commands...but we do not pay any attention to
them, not because of willful disobedience but because we
do not love and respect Him."[10]

Remember Zaccheus, the first-century tax
collector? Even more so than now, tax collectors in the
first century were despised and deeply resented. They
were representatives of the occupying Roman state that
levied heavy taxes on the people of Israel. It was not
uncommon to hear of a Jewish tax collector who would
demand double of the people, giving half to Rome and
keeping half for himself. These men became rich by
ripping off their own people, and they were hated for
their deception.

There Zaccheus was, up in a tree, trying to catch
a glimpse of Jesus. Jesus saw him and, rather than treat

---

10 - Chambers, O. (1992). *My Utmost for His Highest.* Grand Rapids, MI:
Discovery House Publishers.

him with disgust as so many others would have, Jesus called him by name and told him to lead the way to his home. Zaccheus obeyed and had an encounter with Jesus that changed his life. In front of all assembled, Zaccheus declared, *Behold, Lord, half of my possessions I will give to the poor, and if I have defrauded anyone of anything, I will give back four times as much* (Luke19:8). Zaccheus knew he had robbed many of the people listening to him. We have no reason to doubt he kept his word and later humbly returned what he had stolen from his neighbors. Can you imagine the impact this had on his community? His restitution probably resulted in a revival.

I read a story a number of years ago about a young girl who needed a kidney transplant. The only donor match was her father, who was happy to help save his daughter's life, but he had a problem: he was one hundred pounds overweight, which threatened his chance of surviving the transplant surgery. In order to give his kidney to his daughter, the father radically changed his eating habits and began to exercise, and over the course of the next year he lost two pounds a week. After his healthy makeover, he was able to successfully donate his kidney to his daughter. How was this father able to accomplish such a remarkable feat? He loved his daughter with his whole heart, soul, and mind. When we love Jesus like this, giving will be a natural outcome.

WE THINK WE CANNOT AFFORD TO GIVE

Many do not give because they think they cannot afford to. Statistics from the Barna Research Group's 1997, 1999, and 2000 reports show that over 90% of American Christian families do not give even ten percent.[11] Many of these feel that giving is out of their budget. However, not being able to afford to give is most often a symptom of other problems, particularly financial mismanagement and lack of planning.

---

11 - Carlson, E. (2003). "Do Worshippers Give God His 10 Percent?" Retrieved from http://oursaviourlutheran.com/story_7322.html

If you told me you could not afford to give, I would ask about your spending habits. Take a look at your bank and/or credit card statements to help you answer the following questions:

How many $5 cups of coffee do you drink a week?

How often do you and your family eat out instead of preparing a less expensive homemade meal?

What does your cable television bill look like each month?

How many car payments do you have? Could you sell your car(s) and purchase older vehicles with cash?

How is your consumer debt? Are you in the process of paying off your credit cards and/or minimizing your debt load?

When you get out of debt, will you be able to afford to give at least ten percent?

Are you using a budget to keep track of how you spend money? If not, how do you know you cannot afford to give?

If you began to budget and kept track of how you spent your money, would you be able to start giving more generously?

Financially derailed people typically operate with no budget and have no idea where their money is going. Additionally, they usually carry a lot of debt and, as a result, have no spare cash. Their inability to give is, thus, self-inflicted. Friend, debt keeps you from giving, but giving will keep you from debt.

You may ask, "What about the widow, the divorced person, or the single parent who is truly unable to give?" I have talked with people who were surviving on as little as $800 a month and yet found ways to give. I am reminded of one such person, a single mother who was able to give $1,260 to a building fund. She was already giving ten percent, but when her church began a building program she wanted to give more. The church asked for pledges, and so this woman canceled her family's cable television so they could contribute $35 a month. This was a sacrifice for this family, but what a lesson in giving the godly mother taught her children!

Under certain circumstances, the Bible does make allowances for not being able to afford to give, but they are not to be used as an excuse not to give. An inability to give is for a season; it is not a lifestyle. I am thinking of the hard worker who loses a job or becomes responsible for the debt of an extended family member, the mother abandoned by a husband who sabotaged the family's finances, and dozens of other similar circumstances. The Christian who finds him or herself in such a situation will be grieved by the inability to give. If this is you, share your heartache with a trusted pastor. He needs to know what is going on. Let him know of your desire to remedy the situation and your intention to get back to the level of giving you practiced in the past.

In the meantime, don't sweat being unable to give what you just don't have. Be glad for whatever amount you can give. Although your portion of giving may be small for a season, you are still sowing bountifully. After all, Jesus is not after your money; He wants the integrity of your heart. In 2 Corinthians 8:12 Paul writes, *For if the readiness is present, it is acceptable according to what a person has, not according to what he does not have.* This is beautiful. You are only responsible to give what you have, not what you do not have.

WE DO NOT TRUST GOD

There are approximately 150 references in the Bible that tell us to trust the Lord. Clearly, trust is an important aspect of the Christian's relationship with God. Consider this: would we have been directed to give ten percent of our income if we could not live—and live well—without it? Yet while the basis of the Christian faith is trusting God with our eternal souls, most of us simply will not or cannot trust Him with our finances.

Think about this for a moment. If you have trusted your life to a God you cannot see, and you believe when you die your soul will go to heaven for eternity, how is it that you do not trust Him for the money you need this week? If you can trust Him for eternity, can't you trust Him until payday?

Recently, in his final message on the topic of stewardship, a pastor told his congregation that if they wanted to begin tithing but were unsure how it might affect their finances, he would offer a money-back guarantee. If after ninety days of tithing and following God's principles they felt they were not in better financial shape, he would refund their money. He knew that while it may not be right, most people find it easier to trust a man than to trust Jesus.

In God we have a much better guarantee than any pastor could offer. The guarantee is found in both the Old and New Testaments. In Malachi 3:10-11, the Lord says,

Bring the whole tithe into the storehouse, so that there may be food in My house, and test Me now in this," says the LORD of hosts, "if I will not open for you the windows of heaven and pour out for you a blessing until it overflows. Then I will rebuke the devourer for you, so that it will not destroy the fruits of the ground; nor will your vine in the field cast its grapes," says the LORD of hosts.

The apostle Paul gives a similar guarantee in the New Testament: *God is able to make all grace abound to you, so that always having all sufficiency in everything, you may have an abundance for every good deed* (2 Corinthians 9:8). Between these promises, we should not need the assurance of a pastor.

WE ARE IGNORANT ABOUT GIVING

One last reason people don't give is that they don't know they are supposed to give. Considering the large number of pastors who are reluctant to teach God's principles about money, such ignorance is not surprising. Maybe pastoral reluctance is due to the fear of man. Maybe churches have misrepresented God in how they present giving, and they have broken people's trust by misspending the money they collect.

In the past, you may not have known what your giving responsibilities were, but you know now. The Bible tells you to give. The choice to obey or not is up to you. But now that you know what is required of you, remember that James 4:17 says, *Therefore, to one who knows the right thing to do and does not do it, to him it is sin.*

The story is told of former president Lyndon Johnson's great-grandfather who, when he was baptized, said, "I want to pay half of the minister's salary." He was asked the reason for this strange request and he answered, "It is very simple. My wallet was baptized, too."

Friend, has your wallet been baptized? Martin Luther astutely observed, "There are three conversions necessary: the conversion of the heart, the mind, and the purse."[12] Of these three, it may be that we modern Christians find the conversion of the purse to be the most difficult of all.

---

12 - MacPhail, B. (2010). *A Generous Church: Sermons by the Reverend Brynn MacPhail*. Retrieved from http://www.reformedtheology.ca/2corinthians9.htm

Chapter 5

GREED

If your spending record were brought before church leadership, would you want to change or edit anything from it? Explain.

Describe how your spending habits harm or help your testimony as a Christian.

Are you transparent about your purchases or do you hide them from those close to you? Why?

Are you coveting anything right now? What is it and why do you desire it?

What spending habits does God want you to confess and forsake?

But it is important to understand that greed is the antithesis of giving.

I can count on one hand the times I have heard a lecture or sermon or read anything substantial about greed or covetousness. In our "Grab all you can, because you only live once!" society, expressing concern about excess, selfishness, and greed is typically passé. But greed is the antithesis of giving. In the Bible we see powerful principles that can shape and protect us even in a modern society. We see how a single sin can adversely impact a nation, a family, or an individual. God takes sin seriously, even in the life of a believer. Take a moment to meditate on the following:

One sin kept Adam and Eve out of the garden.

One sin kept Moses out of the Promised Land.

One sin cost Samson his sight.

One sin cost Saul his kingdom.

One sin cost Esau his birthright.

One sin cost the life of Lot's wife.

One sin ravaged David's family.

One sin killed Ananias and Sapphira.

One of our sins sent Jesus Christ to the cross.

It has been said, "For want of a nail, the shoe

was lost. For want of a shoe, the horse was lost. For want of a horse, the soldier was lost. For want of a soldier, the battle was lost."[13] How much is lost from God's kingdom for want of funds selfishly spent elsewhere?

GREED IS NOT A PRIVATE SIN

The book of Joshua shows that when greed goes unchecked, judgment and destruction may be brought upon God's people. It also shows us that God sees one man's sin and greed as a nation's sin and greed. Scripture say:

But the sons of Israel acted unfaithfully in regard to the things under the ban, for Achan...took some of the things under the ban, therefore the anger of the LORD burned against the sons of Israel...So the Lord said to Joshua, "Israel has sinned, and they have also transgressed My covenant which I commanded them. And they have even taken some of the things under the ban and have both stolen and deceived. Moreover, they have also put them among their own things." Joshua 7:1, 10-11

When Achan sinned, Israel sinned. God declared the nation guilty, and His anger burned against them. Many Christians feel they can spend their money any way they want as long as they don't hurt anyone. But as Paul says in Romans 14:7, *For not one of us lives for himself, and not one dies for himself.* Our lives as believers are inextricably linked with the lives of those around us. What we do individually affects other believers collectively, tainting others' opinions of all Christians. Scripture warns, *Accordingly, whatever you have said in the dark will be heard in the light, and what you have whispered in the inner rooms will be proclaimed upon the housetops* (Luke 12:3).

Our actions can also affect those closest to us. Out of fear Abraham deceived Pharaoh by hiding the

---

13 - MacPhail, B. (2010). *A Generous Church: Sermons by the Reverend Brynn MacPhail.* Retrieved from http://www.reformedtheology.ca/2corinthians9.htm

fact that Sarah was his wife, and this deception caused destruction in Pharaoh's house and nearly destroyed a nation (Genesis 12). Years later, Abraham's son Isaac followed in his father's footsteps, lying and causing similar problems (Genesis 26:1-17). David had a problem with lust, and his son Amnon later lusted after and raped his half-sister Tamar (2 Samuel 13). Sin, including greed, exposes others to danger and harm.

GREED IS NEVER HIDDEN FROM GOD

In God's eyes, there is no such thing as a secret sin. Something might be concealed from man, but it is always revealed to God:

For My eyes are on all their ways; they are not hidden from My face; nor is their iniquity concealed from My eyes. Jeremiah 16:17

You *have placed our iniquities before You, our secret sins in the light of Your presence.* Psalm 90:8

For God will bring every act to judgment, everything which is hidden, whether it is good or evil. Ecclesiastes 12:14

God hates greed, and He will *bring every act to judgment.* The tragic ending of Ananias and Sapphira exemplifies this spiritual certitude perhaps better than any other biblical story (See pages 162-169). Their greed could not be hidden from God, and the consequences of that greed were compounded by their lies; the Holy Spirit struck both Ananias and Sapphira dead on the spot.

A DEADLY SIN

Greed is considered one of the seven deadly sins and seldom operates in isolation; usually, greed is combined with other sins such as lust, pride, or envy. Greed is not always manifested through the accumulation of money or possessions. Anytime a person strives to receive more than their fair share, or possesses a fanatical desire to accumulate things at the expense of others, it becomes greed. Hoarding is the extreme example of where greed can lead.

Greed is not always blatant; sometimes it assumes subtle forms. When a family member hides the recently baked chocolate chip cookies in a secret place so no one else can eat them, that is greed. When a coworker arrogantly takes credit for the hard work of others, that is greed. When a salesman pads his company expense account to provide for lavish meals and lodging, puts gas in his personal car with the company credit card, and claims these extravagances are simply business charges, that is both greed and stealing. When a trucker refuses to pay his income taxes because he wants to spend more money fixing up his rig, that is greed and stealing.

In summation, any decision made to take from others or to enrich ourselves at the expense of others is greed, which is sin.

BEWARE OF THE SNARE

Dishonest gain is a form of greed, whether it is accomplished quietly or through the use of physical force. Remember, God hates all forms of greed! His commandment clearly states, *Thou shalt not steal* (Exodus 20:15, NJV).

Misers may act out their greed by refusing to spend what they already have, while covetous people incessantly crave more possessions; both are motivated by greed and the desire to accumulate. Paul instructs Timothy to warn wealthy Christians to beware of the snare of riches, and to fight off their seductive power through gracious giving:

*Instruct those who are rich in this present world not
to be conceited or to fix their hope on the uncertainty
of riches, but on God, who richly supplies us with all
things to enjoy. Instruct them to do good, to be rich in
good works, to be generous and ready to share, storing
up for themselves the treasure of a good foundation for
the future, so that they may take hold of that which is
life indeed.* 1 Timothy 6:17–19

Conversely, Scripture warns,

*You shall not covet your neighbor's house; you shall
not covet your neighbor's wife or his male servant or
his female servant or his ox or donkey or anything that
belongs to your neighbor.* Exodus 20:17

THREE FORMS OF GREED

FORM ONE

An obsessive desire for more and more
possessions and the desire for power and prestige. In this
form, earthly goods are a means to an end: the money,
the mansions, the luxury cars are things used to achieve,
wield, and display personal power and prestige. These
things serve to reinforce the collector's illusions about
what is important and to build up a feeling of success.

One way to defeat the desire for power is to be
generous in granting power to others. Avoid jobs that are
a temptation for a power grab. Share credit for successes
with others and claim a fair share of responsibility for
failures being blamed on others.

FORM TWO

A fearful need to store up surplus goods for a
vaguely defined time of want. Fear is a poor motivator
for virtue but an excellent one for greed. Sometimes,
greed is a driving desire to have so much that we believe

we cannot possibly run out. The belief here is that if one acquires enough stock, real estate, or T-bills, he/she will be safe and secure from want. That is an illusion!

There is no perfect preventative for want. There are countless examples of men being millionaires one year and broke the next. In fact, God challenges us to trust in Him, not in our riches.

Some trust in chariots and some in horses, but we trust in the name of the Lord our God. Psalm 20:7, NIV

One cure for this form of greed is to learn to be content with less of the world's goods. Instead of purchasing a brand new car, purchase one a year old. Yes, you will forfeit experiencing that new car smell, but you will save plenty from not taking a hit on the first year of depreciation. Someone once said, "Live simply so that others may simply live." Once this kind of freedom is practiced, the fear of not having possessions is lessened and is replaced by an inner strength and confidence in Him.

FORM THREE

A desire for more and more earthly goods for their own sake. This is slavery to things, plain and simple. We can reduce ourselves to accumulating more electronic gear, trading cards, antiques, or other collectibles. In these cases, our possessions start to own us. The obvious cure for this form of greed is to start reducing the compulsive collection of things so as not to be bound by these material possessions. Do you see the contrast?

Greed is focused on you. It is self-centered and can only offer temporary satisfaction, but no longterm contentment, since you will always want more.

Living an other-centered life puts your focus on

others, and as you strive to bless others, God will in turn find ways to send His blessings and riches (both material and eternal) into your live. Which focus do you desire?

GREED ALWAYS FOLLOWS THE SAME PATTERN

The book of James teaches, *But each one is tempted when he is carried away and enticed by his own lust. Then when lust has conceived, it gives birth to sin; and when sin is accomplished, it brings forth death*"(1:14-15). In 2 Samuel 11:1-17, when David sins with Bathsheba, we can see this progressive pattern in action:

He saw beautiful Bathsheba.

He coveted her.

He took her.

He concealed his sin.

He suffered for his sin.

Achan followed the same pattern of sin:

He saw a garment and gold.

He coveted these items.

He took them.

He concealed the items.

He suffered for his sin.

We are hardly better in modern society. We are bombarded daily, through interactions with others and through media advertising, with things we are told we must have in order to increase our status or appeal or to dispel the notion that somehow we are not and do not yet have enough. We see these things, and too often we rationalize buying or procuring them no matter the financial or personal cost to satisfy our pride. We think, "I deserve it!" And for a short time afterwards, we might even fancy ourselves happier, but that happiness never lasts long. Soon, we are dissatisfied again and looking for the next new thing. Our greed always brings us back for more.

One woman I know was so greedy when it came to shopping that she would buy something over budget, hide it in her closet, and bring it out after a week or two. If her husband asked about it, she just told him she'd bought it some time ago. Greed caused her to rationalize, deceive, and undermine her husband's authority. The suffering she endured was in the form of marital discord, as the two fought constantly over finances. That marriage ended unhappily not many years later.

GREED MUST BE CONFESSED AND FORSAKEN

In Joshua 7:12-13, God says, *I will not be with you anymore unless you destroy the things under the ban from your midst...You cannot stand before your enemies until you have removed the things under the ban from your midst.* God gets very personal here. We have to deal with greed in our own lives. God may use other people to show areas that need change, but we must be the ones who do the changing. Other people cannot change for us.

It is difficult for human beings to curb greed. To submit to Christ's financial lordship goes against our self-interest, pride, and rebellious nature. It goes against human nature to admit we are wrong or that we make mistakes. We hate to admit it when we buy on impulse rather than on a planned budget or that we've put frivolous items on a credit card, purchasing from greed rather than need. With God's help, we have to take responsibility for our sin and turn away from it. Achan was confronted with his own greed and, at the cost of his own life, he took responsibility for his actions:

Truly, I have sinned against the LORD, the God

of Israel Joshua 7:20. His confession was specific and honest—"I saw," "I coveted," "I took," and "I concealed" (21).

Achan did not beat around the bush or rationalize his sin. His specific, honest confession of greed had three powerful results. First, it glorified God; Joshua exhorted Achan, *Give glory to the LORD, the God of Israel. (Joshua 7:19)* Second, it was followed by praise to God. Finally, Achan's confession of greed brought healing and peace to the community. Although he did not live to become a generous giver—Achan and his family were executed in the Valley of Achor— his confession of greed relieved him of sin and brought restoration to the people of Israel.

The end of this story is dire, but the point is that confession is vital to prevent our sins from consuming us from the inside and destroying those around us. As King David knew, the only cure for sin sickness is confession to God: *For I confess my iniquity; I am full of anxiety because of my sin* (Psalm 38:18). Friend, if greed has a hold on your heart, confess it now to the Lord. Keeping silent about this deadly sin causes a great deal of emotional strain and anxiety. Do not carry this burden. Let God restore you and begin to expand your heart.

Chapter 6

WHEN WE FORGET GOD

Are you continuing to grow
spiritually? Why or why not?

How have you forgotten
God in your finances?
In your giving?

Are you making good use
of your time each day?
How could you grow in this
area?

In what area of your
finances do you think God
wants you to consider your
ways?

Where do you need
financial courage?

Where is God shaking your
world to get your attention?

The Israelites started out with great enthusiasm and excitement.

What happens when God's people become so wrapped up in their own lives and agendas that they forget God? The rebuilding of the temple is an instructive story because it shows the importance of finishing well and keeping our priorities—God's priorities—ever before us.

Along the way in our giving, we sometimes get lost, forget our destination, give up because we are tired, or lose heart because the way is difficult. As we see in the book of Ezra, this problem is not unique to contemporary believers. In Ezra 2 we learn that 42,360 exiled Jews, held captive in Babylon for seventy years, were called by King Cyrus back to Jerusalem. Not only were they going home but they were doing so with a purpose given and empowered by God: they were going to rebuild the temple.

The temple played a far more significant role in the ancient Jewish culture than today's churches do in our society. It served as a place of worship, teaching, social interaction, community life, and training. Here the people met God and each other, here they married and buried, and here they passed on their teachings, traditions, customs, and culture. The temple was sacred. Under the evil reign of King Zedekiah, God's temple had been decimated and abandoned for seventy years, and when the people returned to Judah from their captivity in Babylon, it was virtually in ruins. But God, through the prophets, called his people back to rebuild the temple.

A GOOD START IN GIVING

Much like many church building projects today, the temple rebuild started well. The Israelites began the work with 42,360 free men and 7,337 servants—plenty of people for the task. In Ezra 2:69, we see financial generosity at the beginning of the project: *According to their ability they gave to the treasury for the work 61,000 gold drachmas, and 5,000 silver minas and 100 priestly garments.* In the next verse, singers are present. In other words, the Israelites started out with great enthusiasm and excitement.

God's anointed prophets were in the thick of the action. Haggai and Zechariah were not just "words in the wind" prophets. They rolled up their sleeves, supporting the workers with their own sweat (Ezra 5:2). Haggai, whose name means "festive,"[14] knew how to have a good time—he found it in obeying God. At this point, the people were enthusiastic about what God was doing in their midst, and they were full of zeal to give wholeheartedly.

ROADBLOCKS AHEAD

Then, they encountered resistance. They allowed that resistance to become a reason to quit giving. Even today, whenever Christians step out in faith, especially in the area of giving, Satan tries to sidetrack our efforts with the same roadblocks he used in Ezra's time:

Ungodly partnerships (Ezra 4:2)

Discouragement (Ezra 4:4)

Fear (Ezra 4:4)

Frustration (Ezra 4:5)

---

14 - "Haggai: Meaning and Etymology." Retrieved from http://www.abarim-publications.com/Meaning/Haggai.html#UFF5qqTybc0

Accusation (Ezra 4:6)

Legal force (Ezra 4:11-15, 23)

These tactics worked. Despite all the effort the people had taken to lay the temple's foundation and erect the altar, they abandoned the project for about 20 years (Ezra 4:23, 6:15).

LET'S KEEP OUR EYES ON JESUS

I once heard a story about a group of four runners who teamed up to compete in an invitational track meet to set a county record. The first two runners did well, and after accepting a perfect baton pass the third runner took off like a bullet. The final runner was poised and in position to blaze the last leg of the race. But halfway through his paces, the third runner slowed then walked off the track onto the grassy center field. His teammates rushed over to him, thinking he had stopped because of an injury, but his answer floored them: "Oh, I just didn't feel like doing it anymore, so I quit."

All too often, just like in Ezra's day, we begin our giving projects with enthusiasm but because of roadblocks we abandon them or finish with less than our best efforts. As we mature in Christ and keep our focus on Him as our example, we learn endurance, develop strength, and maintain vision in our giving. Like athletes, we have to press on toward the high calling of God and never give up (Philippians 3:14; Galatians 6:9).

THE ROADBLOCK OF SELF-INTEREST

Do you remember when you were first saved? God was your top priority. You were going to single-handedly win the world for Christ. Talking to God was the best part of your day, and you did it often. But as the months and years passed, you became too self-involved even to remember to say a blessing over the food in a restaurant. Initially generous with your time, talents, and money, with time you began to let your own self-interest get in the way of your giving. You sit in the church pews each week and, forgetting God's purposes, wait to be served rather than to serve (Matthew 20:28).

Many Christians start well in financial generosity to the Lord, but this largess is not generally long lived. Like the people of Judah, the majority of American Christians have turned their backs on what matters to God: reconciling the world to Himself.

In Haggai 1:4, the prophet hits the nail right on the head: *Is it time for you yourselves to dwell in your paneled houses while this house lies desolate?"*Wow. Let those words sink in for a moment and give thought to this: in those days, only the wealthy would have been able to afford paneled houses. Imagine the reaction of these affluent Israelites. What would we do to our preachers if they confronted us like Haggai did?

Haggai accuses the people of Judah of being generous with themselves but not with God. Where are the time and resources for God's work that they have so generously spent on themselves? The dichotomy is not only glaring but gross. The people of Judah have neither time nor money for the temple, but plenty of both for their own houses.

By way of comparison, according to researchers, Christian giving in America is at a lower percentage now than it was during the Great Depression. Think about that for a moment. During that era it was common to be without a job or ample food to avoid starvation, yet the average member of a Protestant church gave 3.3% of his or her income for the work of God. This means that as a nation, America was more generous in 1921 than in the year 2000, when, despite enjoying healthy economic conditions and years of abundance, Protestant church members gave 2.6% of their income and donated an average of $17 per person each week.[15]

We see a similar pattern in giving after the economic crisis of 2008. According to surveys conducted by the Barna Group, 20% of Americans reduced their giving to churches in late 2008 in response to economic pressures, by 2010 that number had increased to 30%, and by 2011, when the country had largely begun to recover, it had not changed.[16] It seems that as a nation we are more generous during times of economic calamity than in times of financial blessing.

Haggai rebukes the Israelites for withholding not only their money but their service as well. Likewise, in any contemporary church, you will find about twenty percent of the people doing eighty percent of the work, just a few faithful people serving week in and week out. I remember being in charge of finding volunteers for the nursery at a small church that my family attended. Countless times I was told, "Why would we serve in the nursery? We don't have kids." Or, "Our kids have grown up. I don't do that anymore." After I had been in other churches a few more years, I found this attitude toward serving was common among Christians. Idealistically, I used to think it would be nice if the mother of young children could have an hour or two to enjoy worship services. Reality showed me these women were the only ones who would volunteer to watch the little ones.

CONSIDER GOD AND HIS WAYS

Haggai challenges this blasé attitude: *Now therefore, thus says the LORD of hosts, "Consider your ways!"* (1:5). Consider means "to deliberate upon, to examine, to study, to set your heart on, to believe after careful deliberation, or to judge."[17] In other words, Haggai is saying, "Hey guys, how are things working out

15 - Ronsvalle, J.L., & Ronsvalle, S. (2002). "The State of Church Giving Through 2000." Champaign, IL: Empty Tomb.
16 - Barna Group (2011). "Donors Proceed with Caution, Tithing Declines." Retrieved from http://www.barna.org
17 - Zodhiates, S. (1992).

for you? How are your finances doing? How are things working in your life? What are the results of you ignoring God's work?" Haggai wanted God's people to look at what happens when they turn their backs on God, forget what is important to Him, and choose to pursue their own priorities at the expense of God's.

Five times Haagai challenges us to "consider" our giving ways. Ask yourself the same questions. Are you ahead yet? Is working all those long hours and living at warp speed paying off? Has ignoring God's Word and neglecting to give generously increased your net worth? Haggai teaches that halfhearted obedience never brings wholehearted blessings. Without obedience to God, there is never enough money or time. The line "I can't get no satisfaction!" from The Rolling Stones' hit song could have been written by Haggai instead of Mick Jagger and Keith Richards. The correlation between obedience to God's Word and His work is this: the more we show that we are faithful with what God has given us to manage, the more He can entrust to us.

This principle of stewardship is also found in Luke 16, where Jesus says if we are faithful with money, we will be faithful with true riches which money cannot buy. Because money is the least we are responsible for, how we manage it is often the first indication that we are on the road to being disciples of Christ.

We have limited time on this planet. There is an appointed time for every event under heaven (Ecclesiastes 3:1), and we make time for what is truly important to us. But too often, God's Word is choked out by the worries of the world and the deceitfulness of riches (Matthew 13:22). Like a swimmer at the beach, you may have started with the shore of God's truth plainly in view, but slowly, almost imperceptibly, you have drifted from shore. We need to consider our ways and ask ourselves whether or not we are applying God's principles to our finances. If not, when are we going to start? Remember, the time for obedience is as soon as we become aware of the principle. James does not mince words: *Therefore, to one who knows the right thing to do and does not do it, to him it is sin.* (James 4:17)

Haggai has more to say to us: *You have sown much, but harvest little; you eat, but there is not enough to be satisfied; you drink, but there is not enough to become drunk; you put on clothing, but no one is warm enough; and he who earns, earns wages to put into a purse with holes* (Haggai 1:6). Though the Israelites worked hard, they had little to show for it. The problem was not that they were lazy but that they seemed to have insatiable appetites. No matter how much they worked, ate, or drank, it was never enough.

Isn't this like us today? If you look around, you will see ambitious people working hard and long at a breakneck pace, just trying to get ahead — but for what? No matter how hard or long we work, many of us are about two paychecks away from living on the street. We think we are sowing a lot, but we are reaping little because we have forgotten God, we have failed to invite Him into our finances. We have taken Him out of the equation.

In the face of discouragement, fear, ungodly partnerships, frustration, and political pressures, the Israelites did not acknowledge that their lack of provision was a judgment for forgetting God and His work; rather, they tried to use their poverty as excuse for not finishing the temple. But Haggai reminds us why they experienced poverty in the first place:

Because of My house which lies desolate, while each of you runs to his own house. Therefore, because of you the sky has withheld its dew and the earth has withheld its produce. I called for a drought on the land, on the mountains, on the grain, on the new wine, on the oil, on

*what the ground produces, on men, on cattle, and on all
the labor of your hands.* Haggai 1:9-11

How can you argue with that? God is mad. He has been
forgotten.

If you have a lifestyle of living paycheck to
paycheck while under constant, intense financial
pressure, it is likely because you've strayed from biblical
financial principles. I realize there are exceptions: people
who do everything right according to biblical principles,
yet for some reason always seem to be struggling. But
many Christians who are struggling financially have
forgotten what God wants. I once heard a speaker say,
"If I could kick the person most responsible for my
problems, I wouldn't be able to sit for a month." Amen
and amen!

We think we are getting ahead by forgetting
about God in our finances, but we are fooling ourselves.
Think about it for a moment: do we know more than
God? Do we believe God has our best interests at heart?
If God knows better than us and has our best interests at
heart, wouldn't it be wise to invite Him into our giving
and spending so we begin to do things His way?

An old southern preacher used to read this poem
to his congregation:

"When God gets His and I get mine, then everything is
just fine. But if I get mine and take God's too, what do
you think God will do? I think He'll collect, don't you?"

I believe God does collect from us. Haggai warns
that if you take what belongs to God and redirect it to
your own resources, somewhere down the line you will
discover that things are not working out for you like you
thought they would.

Let me close this chapter with a look at how

Haggai's words can revitalize your life as you remember God in your finances:

God will be with you (Haggai 2:4-5).

God will fill your house with wealth & glory (2:7).

God will give you peace as you obey (2:9).

God will bless you with His provision (2:19).

The catch is that you have to make the first move. You cannot be like the people of Israel who did not feel the time was right to give. The time for giving is now. Haggai knew that giving takes fortitude and strength. He told the governor, priest, and people to take courage (Haggai 2:4). Obedience to God cannot depend on how we feel. You and I will not feel like being obedient to anything until we begin to do it.

Do we feel like remembering what God has said and living by godly financial principles? Do we feel like waiting until we can afford to pay for something before we buy it? Do we feel like giving to God consistently and generously? No, we do not—at least not initially. We do not start to feel like giving until we enjoy the fruit of living without that nagging consumer debt hanging over us or until we have experienced living without financial pressure. We do not enjoy feeling right about giving to God until we give long enough to experience the great joy that obedience to God's Word produces in us.

How did things turn out for the people after they were obedient to Haggai's message? Haggai 1:14 reports the happy ending:

So the LORD stirred up the spirit of Zerubbabel the son of Shealtiel, governor of Judah, and the spirit of Joshua the son of Jehozadak, the high priest, and the spirit of all the remnant of the people; and they came and worked on the house of the LORD of hosts, their God.

Ezra 6:14-16 continues the story:

> *And the elders of the Jews were successful in building through the prophesying of Haggai the prophet and Zechariah the son of Iddo. And they finished building according to the command of the God of Israel and the decree of Cyrus, Darius, and Artaxerxes king of Persia. This temple was completed on the third day of the month Adar... And the sons of Israel, the priests, the Levites and the rest of the exiles, celebrated the dedication of this house of God with joy.*

Remember that blessing follows obedience. We simply cannot neglect God's priorities and God's Word and expect to be prosperous and successful—at least, not for long. Haggai reminds us, *"The silver is Mine, and the gold is Mine," declares the LORD of hosts* (2:8). It is as if God is saying to us, "I have entrusted money, time, and talents to you. Use them wisely on My behalf. If you are a faithful steward, I will bless you and give you more."

Chapter 7

GIVING PATTERNS
FROM THE BIBLE

Have you ever given even when it was a real sacrifice for you?

Have you ever given through other ways than money?

Is there any area in your giving or even in your life where you show a lack of trust in God?

Do you give below your ability? At your ability? Or, do you give beyond your ability?

The Bible illustrates key giving principles that are as relevant today as they were when they were written.

Now that we know *why* we should give, it is important to discover *how* we are to go about giving of our tithes and offerings. For this we can turn again to the Bible, which, through stories of people whose giving and lifestyles truly pleased God, can illustrate key giving principles that are as relevant today as they were then.

The next pages highlight significant moments in the lives of Eliezer, the Widow of Zarephath, Mary, and others. Several principles of godly giving can be gleaned from these examples:

Share God's blessings: Some of those we'll read about were compelled to give by an overwhelming gratefulness for the goodness of God and His blessings in their lives; all were blessed as a result of their giving.

Have a servant's heart: One common characteristic of all those whose stories follow is their humility and willingness to serve, whether literally or through their giving acts (Mary).

Give even if the recipient cannot reciprocate: We are to be *Shrewd as serpents and innocent as doves* (Matthew 10:16) in our finances as in other areas of our lives, but there may be times we are called to give even when the recipient has no power to return what we have given. Christians are called to be generous toward those in need. When we obey this call, God can bless us through churches, businesses, or countless other means. He never overlooks the good we do for others in His name.

GIVING AS SACRIFICE: THE WIDOW'S MITE

The Bible does not only contain examples of people who gave out of their surplus, it also provides examples of those who gave even when giving was a real sacrifice for them and their family. Take a look at the pattern set two thousand years ago by a poor Jewish widow, whose giving was noticed by Jesus:

And He sat down opposite the treasury, and began observing how the people were putting money into the treasury; and many rich people were putting in large sums. A poor widow came and put in two small copper coins, which amount to a cent. Calling His disciples to Him, He said to them, "Truly I say to you, this poor widow put in more than all the contributors to the treasury; for they all put in out of their surplus, but she, out of her poverty, put in all she owned, all she had to live on." Mark 12:41-44

It should be sobering to realize Jesus sees not only what we give, but also what we withhold. He saw that the widow *put in more than all the contributors to the treasury, for they all put in out of their surplus.* I daresay most of the giving we do in America is out of our abundance, but Jesus reveals it is not the portion but the proportion that is important. The widow put in two coins, equal to one sixty-fourth of an average worker's daily wage, but for her this small sum was everything. She kept nothing for herself.

It is no coincidence that one of Jesus' last public acts of ministry was not performing a miracle or healing an illness, but observing people's giving habits. Jesus zeroed in on the widow's humble act of giving, laying out a pattern for us to follow.

He tells us the first step of Christian discipleship is to give all. Just before the widow put her coins into the treasury, Jesus was asked by one of the scribes, *What commandment is the foremost of all?* (Mark 12:28). Jesus responded, *You shall love the Lord your God with all your heart, and with all your soul, and with all your mind, and with all your strength* (v. 30). The widow's gift demonstrated who she truly loved.

THE CHURCH

The paradox Jesus noted of the poor widow's meager but sacrificial giving compared with the scant giving of the wealthy continues today. According to U.S. Bureau of Labor Statistics surveys, the poorest 20% of Americans are consistently more generous than the wealthiest 20%, contributing an average of 4.3% of their incomes in 2007 compared with the 2.1% given by the wealthiest Americans.[18]

I know of a church that, due to a lack of generosity, struggled to pay for its building program and two staff salaries. The elders, largely a group of conservative business minds with little faith, decided they should let the associate pastor go and put his salary toward the building program. One of the elders, a senior citizen on a fixed retirement income, stood up to his colleagues. He had a deep biblical faith and believed that the same God who had called their associate pastor to the church would also provide for their needs. He told the elders, "Even though I'm on a fixed income, I will increase my giving to help keep our associate pastor on staff. If we all do this, the church will follow our example and God will indeed bless us. Let's put Him to the test, as He says, and see Him open the windows of heaven and pour out His blessings."

---

18 - U.S. Dept. of Labor (2010). Consumer Expenditure Survey, 2006-2007. Retrieved from www.bls.gov/cex/twoyear/200607/csxtwoyr.pdf

Eventually the others begrudgingly decided to give towards meeting the associate pastor's needs, but they were willing to give only out of their surplus. For a while afterward, the associate pastor took on a second job at a local restaurant so he could meet his financial needs. When the elders came in to dine, they were too embarrassed and ashamed to even acknowledge him. Imagine what might have happened and how many more lives could have been reached if these men of God had acted in faith instead of unbelief!

Jim Elliot, the Christian missionary martyred in Ecuador in 1956, once said, "He is no fool who gives what he cannot keep in order to gain what he cannot lose."[19] He and his fellow missionaries were massacred trying to establish contact with the Auca Indians in Ecuador. His widow remained in Ecuador, continuing to spread the Gospel. As a result of the Christ-led sacrificial giving of these missionaries, the Aucas and other tribes came to the Lord, and hundreds of young people flocked to the mission field. Books were written and the movies *Beyond the Gates of Splendor* and *The End of the Spear* have told the world this story.

FINAL LESSONS FROM THE WIDOW'S PATTERN

There are two final lessons to be grasped here. First is a lesson for the wealthy, who, because of greed and a desire for luxury, give little to God and the poor. Jesus rebukes such selfishness and calls those who have plenty to give in humility.

Second is a lesson of faith for those who are poor. Too often they give nothing in their poverty because they fear not having enough to live on. In holding back from God, they show a lack of trust in the Lord. The widow's giving was motivated by neither selfishness nor fear. In her giving, she demonstrated contentment and trust in the Lord, which are absolute

---

19 - Elliot, E. (1958). *In the Shadow of the Almighty.* New York: Harper and Row.

requirements for maturity in Christ.

GIVING AS STEWARDSHIP: ELIEZER

I think we often undervalue the importance of giving in our lives because we don't fully understand how stewardship is linked to an intimate relationship with God. We tend to see stewardship as a system practiced by the church to extract money from us. While applying proper stewardship principles includes giving money to the local church, limiting stewardship practices to money is a very narrow understanding of the biblical concept. Stewardship involves arranging our whole lives so as to please the Lord. A steward constantly asks the question, "Lord, what do You want me to do with what You've entrusted to me?"

The Hebrew word translated as steward in the King James Bible is "mesheq", which means "son of possession." Elsewhere in this translation, steward is used for Hebrew words that mean "man," "governor," "keeper," and "servant."[20] A steward was a man placed in charge of managing another's goods or estate. This responsibility required depth of character, intimate knowledge of and commitment to the master, and the ability to wisely handle the master's affairs.

In Genesis 24 we meet an exemplary steward: Eliezer, the Damascene. Eliezer was Abraham's trusted chief servant. Before the birth of his sons Ishmael and Isaac, Abraham also adopted the steward as his sole heir (Genesis 15:2-3). This was a testament to the wisdom, skill, and integrity Eliezer brought to his role as steward. The pattern set by this humble servant reveals invaluable principles for us.

TRUSTWORTHINESS AND ACCOUNTABILITY

After many years, when Abraham was very old and wished to secure his family's future, he turned

---

20 - Zodhiates, S. (1992).

to his oldest and most trusted servant to handle the task. He had already trusted Eliezer with his estate. Now Abraham entrusted to Eliezer his most treasured possession: his son. He asked Eliezer to return to Haran, Abraham's homeland, and find a suitable wife for Isaac.

Abraham's final recorded words show him charging Eliezer to find his son's future bride. Abraham wrote out a list of all his fortune and gave it to Eliezer to show to the prospective in-laws. Then he made a covenant oath with Eliezer, an oath revocable only if Eliezer carried out all of Abraham's wishes but was unable to find a bride for Isaac. Think about this for a moment. Abraham put the deed to his entire estate into Eliezer's hand to take with him on a task that only someone trusted above all others could carry out.

STEWARDSHIP DEMANDS AVAILABILITY

First, Eliezer was available to his master. He did not try to get out of his assignment but immediately began preparing for the trip, readying ten of Abraham's camels and a wealth of valuable possessions. As a hardworking steward managing the estate of one of the wealthiest men in the known world at that time, Eliezer's schedule was undoubtedly already full. The prospect of taking a long, hard trip to find a woman he had never met could not have seemed convenient or attractive. But this steward understood that his first responsibility was to be available to do as his master wished. As Eliezer was available to his master, so are we to be available to God.

STEWARDSHIP DEMANDS COMMITMENT

Not only was Eliezer available, but he was also eager to fulfill Abraham's wishes. His only concerns about the task given to him were about how he would best be able to please his master. To Eliezer's credit, Abraham had complete confidence in the plan and in his steward's ability to fulfill it. This is a great example of stewardship.

Many organizations search in vain for employees (stewards) who are eager to please and committed to their jobs. Eliezer's example is even more remarkable considering that, due to the births of Ishmael and Isaac, he essentially lost what would have been the biggest promotion of his life, yet he still carried out his duties faithfully and honorably, aiming to please his master in all of his actions.

Considering how valued and trusted Eliezer was, I find it intriguing that Abraham took the extra step of asking Eliezer to swear an oath (Genesis 24:9), but Eliezer did not take offense because he had already committed in his heart to serve Abraham. Only those who are not completely committed to honoring an agreement will be offended by having to affirm that commitment on a dotted line.

STEWARDSHIP DEMANDS PRAYERFUL PLANNING

In Genesis 24:12, Eliezer prays for success in carrying out his momentous task: *He said, "O LORD, the God of my master Abraham, please grant me success today, and show lovingkindness to my master Abraham."* This prayer shows Eliezer's understanding of the importance of looking to God for divine guidance, lifting up his needs in prayer, and then listening to whatever God directs him to do.

The plan that Eliezer crafted to help him accomplish the task of choosing Isaac's wife demanded his reliance on God's direction. First, he carefully outlined the characteristics and behaviors of the woman who would be Isaac's wife. Then he had to be silent and wait, watch, and listen for God's answer: *Before they call, I will answer; while they are still speaking, I will hear* (Isaiah 65:24). Thus, when a girl named Rebekah met every prerequisite on Eliezer's list, he was able to say with confidence, *The LORD has guided me* (Genesis 24:27).

FOLLOW THE GIVING PATTERN OF ELIEZER

Eliezer's life is a beautiful picture of the way we are to approach stewardship. He was accountable, available, committed, and prayerful. His life was lived with the singular purpose of managing Abraham's affairs with integrity and wisdom. He was valued and trusted enough to be given responsibility for all of his master's estate. Likewise, as Christians we have the responsibility of caring for God's estate.

Being a steward is not a matter of simply giving God ten percent of your money and doing whatever you like with the rest. It means realizing that God owns everything, so we are responsible to Him for every decision we make with the resources He has entrusted to us.

ISRAELITES' FIRST FRUITS GIVING

Templates are guides that help us stay true to a set pattern. They are used in fashion design, artistic lettering, construction, and many other fields. Throughout Scripture, God has laid out practical templates to help us keep Him first in our lives. The Old Testament feasts are some of these memorable patterns that point to the importance of making God the focal point of our lives.

One such template is the feast of the first fruits. In Deuteronomy 26 (and also Leviticus 23), the Lord instructs His people to keep Him first and foremost by giving the first portion of whatever they produce:

Then it shall be, when you enter the land which the LORD your God gives you as an inheritance, and you

possess it and live in it, that you shall take some of the
first of all the produce of the ground which you shall
bring in from your land that the LORD your God gives
you, and you shall put it in a basket and go to the place
where the LORD your God chooses to establish His
name. You shall go to the priest who is in office at that
time and say to him, "I declare this day to the LORD my
God that I have entered the land which the LORD swore
to our fathers to give us." Then the priest shall take the
basket from your hand and set it down before the altar
of the LORD your God. You shall answer and say before
the LORD your God... "Now behold, I have brought the
first of the produce of the ground which You, O LORD
have given me." And you shall set it down before the
LORD your God, and worship before the LORD your
God. Deuteronomy 26:1-5, 10

FIRST FRUITS GIVING: A DELIBERATE DECISION

This passage provides several principles about
giving. First, giving your first and best fruits requires a
deliberate decision on your part. Notice the Israelites'
entry into the land of inheritance is assumed as when,
not if. In other words, their obedience is expected. Then
they are instructed to "take," "bring," and "put" a portion
of the first fruits of their produce to give to God. Implied
is the understanding that in so doing they will be putting
God first in their lives, and they will remember that
everything they have comes from Him.

Historically, as long as the Israelites did
this God blessed them. Once they began to neglect
His instructions, they fell into sin, moral decay, and
eventually a 70-year captivity. The book of Nehemiah
reveals that one of the first things the Israelites
re-established after their release was their first fruits
giving.

First fruits giving is a good pattern to follow in

our giving today. When we put God first in our lives, He blesses us. But too often we give Him lip service without being deliberate in our giving. Our devotion slips. Before long, God is at the bottom of the heap.

DEFINITE AND DIRECTED

Second, we learn that giving our first fruits should take a definite direction. The Israelites were told to take their offering *to the place where the LORD your God chooses to establish His name (Deuteronomy 26:2).* Where to give hard-earned financial resources should not be an arbitrary decision but should be directed to where God's presence is in our lives: the local church.

A DEMONSTRATIVE DECLARATION

With the phrase *"I declare this day,"* the first fruits giver proclaims that God has kept His word and has brought him into the land promised to his fathers, a land *flowing with milk and honey* (Exodus 3:17). Because of God's faithfulness, the giver worships before the Lord. In a similar way, our giving declares to Christians, non-Christians, and even angelic hosts in Heaven and demons in Hell that God can be counted on to keep His promises.

PUT FIRST THINGS FIRST

Some say, "I'd like to be faithful in my giving. I know this means I should give the first portion of what I earn to the Lord, but that just doesn't make any sense at all. I'm not even making it on 100% of what I earn right now, so how in the world am I supposed to make it on anything less?"

If we rely on our own reasoning and withhold our giving until after we have sorted out our finances, we will never get very far in our giving. Our faith will not grow, and our money will disappear from our wallets. We must learn to give as God gives: freely and without reserve. After all, from a human perspective, it also does not make a lot of sense that *God so loved the world, that He gave His only begotten Son, that whoever believes in Him shall not perish, but have eternal life* (John 3:16). Why does God give so much to us? How are we to respond?

As I believe and act upon God's promises in every realm of my Christian walk, I discover that when God gets involved, He always takes me to a higher level of maturity, one with more potential and possibility than anything my puny human understanding can imagine. If I am willing to follow Him when His instructions seem illogical, He unfailingly demonstrates His faithfulness.

Many who follow the pattern of first fruits giving share testimony after testimony of how, through the years, God has provided *far more abundantly beyond all that we ask* (Ephesians 3:20). It is wonderful to see God work in our lives when we have an unexpected need.

In the Sermon on the Mount, Jesus says we should not worry about what we are going to wear or what we are going to eat. He says, *But seek first His kingdom and His righteousness, and all these things will be added to you* (Matthew 6:33). Put first things first. Move God to the top of your priority list and see how He provides for you. When God allows you to earn a living (supplying you with the necessary energy, skill, and opportunity), remember it is He who provides for you and your family, not you.

Do not wait until other obligations and expenditures exhaust your financial resources. Sit down and say, "I'm going to give God the first fruits of all I earn and put him in the #1 position in my life." If money is an issue, pray about it. If you say you're depending upon God but you don't pray, you are not telling the truth. Prayer is the evidence of your dependence upon God.

It is dishonest to say, "God is first in my life," and then ignore the giving part of your life with Him. If he has been at the bottom of our priority list, where should we expect to be on His? But thank God that He is faithful despite our faithlessness.

GIVING IN FAITH

ELIJAH AND THE WIDOW OF ZAREPHATH

The Old Testament story of Elijah and the widow of Zarephath also demonstrates the power of putting first things first and giving all in faith. In 1 Kings, a poor widow with a young son is asked to give all she has in faith to God's servant Elijah. Although this makes no sense to her and it may even endanger her family, she obeys and is blessed beyond her wildest dreams. As we follow her pattern of obedient giving we will experience God's blessings.

We read in 1 Kings 17:8-9: *Then the word of the LORD came to [Elijah], saying, "Arise, go to Zarephath, which belongs to Sidon, and stay there; behold, I have commanded a widow there to provide for you."* Sidon was a formidable hundred miles away from where Elijah was. There was famine in the land. Plus, it was the city of the Phoenicians, the center of Baal worship. If I were Elijah, I would be checking my marching orders to see whether or not I had read the instructions right. I would be saying to God, "Seriously? Sidon? You're going to do what and provide for me how?"

Often, God's direction does not make sense to any human way of reasoning. If you or I had planned this out for Elijah, we certainly would not have suggested such a route. The prophet's natural instincts would be to abhor the thought of going into a hotbed of Baal worship and to shrink from being a burden upon a poor widow. But that is exactly what God told him to do. If you think the story is illogical up to this point, hold on; it gets even more interesting. Elijah obeys God, as we read in 1 Kings 17:10-12:

So he arose and went to Zarephath, and when he came to the gate of the city, behold, a widow was there gathering sticks; and he called to her and said, "Please get me a little water in a jar, that I may drink." As she was going to get it, he called to her and said, "Please bring me a piece of bread in your hand." But she said, "As the LORD your God lives, I have no bread, only a handful of flour in the bowl and a little oil in the jar; and behold, I am gathering a few sticks that I may go in and prepare for me and my son, that we may eat it and die."

We are not privy to what was going through Elijah's mind at this time. It may have been, "Did I hear God right? Is this how He's going to care for me?" But Elijah's obedience and faith in God's provision is inspiring: *Then Elijah said to her, "Do not fear; go, do as you have said, but make me a little bread cake from it first and bring it to me, and afterward you may make one for yourself and for your son"* 1 Kings 17:13.

The widow must have also been wondering what was going on because she had just explained to Elijah that her flour barrel was dry, she had only a tiny measure of oil left, and she was going to make one last meal for herself and her son. Then, she figured they would wait to die. Elijah answered her, "Fine, but make me a cake first."

Is this the way you have felt about giving to God? You have a pile of bills and responsibilities, and somebody says, "Put God first. Give to God." And you think, "That is the most illogical thing I have ever heard in my life!" But if you read this story carefully, you will discover principles about giving that will help you as they have me. Many Christians today already know that when they put God first by giving Him the first ten percent (or tithe) of what He entrusts to them, He is always there to meet their needs. If you are new to Christianity and have never trusted God in this area of your life, you might be saying, "There is no way this could ever work. God's way just doesn't make sense. It seems foolish!"

Friend, remember that God's foolishness is wiser than man's wisdom (1 Corinthians 1:25). The example of the widow of Zarephath shows us four principles about giving in faith that can encourage us to grow in our giving.

GIVING IN FAITH:

1 - IS A DEATHBLOW TO A SPIRIT OF POVERTY

When Elijah meets the widow in a land plagued by famine, she only has a handful of grain and a tiny bit of oil. For weeks she has been watching the level of flour go down in her barrel. Now she is up against a wall with no hope, no help, and no resources. She has a spirit of poverty. Her provider is right in front of her, yet all she can see is death.

Elijah knows something she does not. He knows that the way to get what you need and live life to the fullest is to put God first. This is why he tells her, "Make me a little cake first."

At the beginning of the story, the widow is clutching onto everything she has, but in the end, she releases it all to God.

There are many people who do not understand that the only way to break a spirit of poverty and truly possess what God has given is to give everything back to God. If you clutch your possessions to yourself, the only thing you will ever have is what you can hold in your hands. If you surrender everything to God with open hands, He will bless you over and above what you had in the first place. Openhanded giving breaks the outer chains of poverty and generates the inner freedom of abundance. When you open your hand to God, He takes what He wills, but He also gives back what you need.

2 - IS A DOWN PAYMENT FOR THE FUTURE

Before the widow gives the first cake to Elijah, she thinks she and her son are about to die. But as she gives in faith, she leaves the future in the hands of God. And get this, friend: God takes care of her.

You may never have had the joy of testing and trusting God with your finances. You may think you cannot afford to give to God first. You may think, "If I didn't have to worry about this bill or that liability, then I could do it." The fact is, the acquisition of more goods does not diminish fear but multiplies it. The more money you have, the more likely you are to hold onto it. If you have not been generous with the little you have, it will be increasingly difficult to put God first when you have more.

In the New Testament, Jesus talked more about money than about Heaven, Hell, or spiritual gifts. Living in us through His Holy Spirit, Jesus understands the human mind as no one ever has before or since. He also knows how prone we are to the faulty reasoning that if only we had a little more money, we would put God first. Yeah, right! Jesus knows it would never work out that way. He knows greed and materialism will always be a problem for anyone who does not put the heavenly Father first.

Some time ago, a woman had one treasure in her life: the silver she had been given on her wedding day. For twenty years, she would nudge her husband at night saying, "John, get up. I think somebody's downstairs, and they're going to get my silver." Her husband would dutifully go check, but there was never anyone there. For years the woman worried, until finally one night the husband went downstairs and surprised a burglar there. Rather than anger, the husband's face expressed relief. He introduced himself to the intruder and said, "Come upstairs and meet my wife. She's been looking for you for twenty years."

Many people are like that. What they have is so important to them that they clutch onto it all the time and cannot think of anything else. They worry about the uncertainty of their financial future and hold tightly to their investments, stocks, property, and savings accounts because they have not put God first.

This sort of chokehold can strangle a Christian's growth. When you put God first and give Him what is rightfully His, you can quit worrying about the future. He will take care of you.

3 - GIVING BY FAITH, NOT BY SIGHT

The Bible says Christians are to walk by faith, not by sight. Giving seems to fly in the face of human reason. The only way to start giving in faith is to respond to what God says in His Word. Cultivate the attitude, "God says it, I believe it, and that settles it." Then, act on this conviction, and give.

This is what the widow of Zarephath had to do. The only word from God she had was Elijah's command to *bring me a little cake first.* She could have reasoned, "I need to take care of my son and myself first," but she understood that Elijah was speaking for God and she obeyed in faith, not because it made sense, not because she figured out how it was going to work, but because God said it.

Elijah gave this woman just one "Thus saith the Lord," and it changed her entire life. Do you know there are about 31,104 verses in the Bible? They contain countless promises from God. This widow was given just one of them. She listened and obeyed, and God honored His word.

Here's the truth: if you are trying to figure out when you will be able to start giving generously based on where you are in your budget, you will never begin. God has said we should give in faith, and in faith is how we should respond. When we put God first in our lives through giving, we pass through the realm of sight and reason and begin to grow and operate in the realm of faith.

4 - ALLOWS GOD TO BLESS THE GIVER

For thus says the LORD God of Israel, "The bowl of flour shall not be exhausted, nor shall the jar of oil be empty, until the day that the LORD sends rain on the face of the earth." So she went and did according to the word of Elijah, and she and he and her household ate for many days. The bowl of flour was not exhausted nor did the jar of oil become empty, according to the word of the LORD which he spoke through Elijah. 1 Kings 17:14-16

Notice the relationship between the widow and God: God spoke, and she responded. The fulfillment of the promise was sure. God did exactly what He said He was going to do.

Look at the blessings that come to the widow after she gives. First, her focus moves from her own plight to that of another in need. Elijah's request for bread stops her cold and stretches her faith even further. Giving out of surplus does not require faith. It is only when we give out of our limited resources that our obedience forces us to trust God to provide an answer to our prayers. As the widow gives what would appear to be her last bit of food, her dire plight turns around.

Imagine the joy in the widow's household when she looks in the barrel each day and there is plenty to sustain the three of them. Also, because she allows the prophet to stay in her home, she is blessed to have God's man right there to pray for her and her family. By faith, the widow puts God first. The result is that God blesses her and meets every one of her needs.

Friend, this is exactly what God has promised to do for you if you put Him first, no matter what.

GOD'S RECIPE FOR GIVING

In this story, four ingredients are blended into a great recipe for giving: God's instruction, our faith, our obedience, and God's blessing. The widow of Zarephath learned how to follow God's prize-winning recipe for giving, which in turn produced abundant life. The widow had a command from God. She followed through in faith, and she obeyed as she was instructed. She put God first, and God went to work on her behalf.

Likewise, we must listen to God's instructions to us for giving. Once we see that God's principles have not changed since the widow's day, we can put faith into our giving. Faith acts as yeast, which is proven by our obedience to the Word. Then comes the blessing. If we try to leave out certain ingredients (withholding faith or obedience), we will not achieve the result of blessing.

APPLYING THE WIDOW'S LESSON TODAY

My wife Julie and I own a landscaping business in San Diego. The business has known many very lean years and many very profitable years. Through it all, we have unwaveringly given far more than a tithe. We discovered long ago that tithing is a wonderful place to start giving, but it is a horrible place to stop. It is our joy to give as much as we can above and beyond our tithe to the Lord's work. We did this when our wages were less than or equal to those of most of our peers, and we have continued to do this during the years our business has prospered.

Friend, day to day we do not know specifically what is going to result from our obedience. The Bible only says we will be blessed if we give; it does not say how or with what we will be blessed. For Julie and I, the what has come in wonderfully surprising ways. During the lean years of our business, our landscaping equipment lasted longer than it should have. We had grown to the point of faith and obedience regarding God's instruction not to purchase depreciating items on credit. We had made a commitment not to borrow to buy equipment, but we had no money to replace items when they wore out. We had a truck that kept running long after it should have collapsed. I well remember push-starting that dilapidated thing so we could get to the next job. It was not pretty, and it was some trouble, but it kept running. I see that as God's hand of blessing on us for our faith and obedience to His instruction.

PROFILE OF A GIVER

A giver does not depend on ability to give or on abundance of wealth. In the case of the widow of Zarephath, the giver was an extremely poor person in a grave situation. The text makes no mention of the widow having any source of income or way to support herself. In Israel, widows and orphans were able to glean (gather) leftover crops from the local harvest to eke out a meager living. But this widow did not live in Israel. She lived in a hostile, foreign land with no welfare system or charity.

Her story demonstrates that a desperate, destitute situation does not negate the biblical requirement to give to God. Not having enough is no excuse. And yet, "not having enough" is exactly the reason Christians offer for why they cannot give. But in the Old Testament, Moses wrote, *Thus all the tithe of the land, of the seed of the land or of the fruit of the tree, is the Lord's; it is holy to the Lord* (Leviticus 27:30). Again, everything we have is really God's, if we manage our money so poorly that we feel unable to afford to tithe, we have spent money that was not ours to spend.

The text shows us we can depend on God when we are obedient to Him and His Word, even when giving under dire circumstances. After we give, we experience blessing. Reaping follows sowing, both in the natural and spiritual realms. In the examples from the Bible, blessing generally follows when believers give, not the other way around. We reap what we sow, after we sow, and more than we sow. That is the law of the harvest (Galatians 6:7-9; James 5:7).

By their actions it seems as if some Christians would rewrite the old hymn "I Surrender All" to say, "One-tenth to Jesus I surrender, one-tenth to Him I'll grudgingly give. I will sometimes love and serve Him, in His presence sometimes live." Friend, we are not at liberty to reinvent God's principles to suit our own self-centered goals. A lifestyle of giving is not based on our circumstances. It is based on having the faith to trust God and the integrity to be obedient to Him.

THE CHURCH'S ATTITUDE TOWARD THE POOR & GIVING

We need to contrast the widow's example with our attitudes about poor people and giving. Many church leaders today seem to have the attitude that the poor have so little to give that their giving could not possibly help anyway. This goes against the teaching of the Lord Jesus Himself. Does a story about a boy with five loaves and two fish ring a bell?

It is a shame when we excuse or even try to stop the poor from giving. First, to do so is to violate Scripture. Second, we do not know how the Lord is going to choose to multiply something. Third, the poor feel needed and have self-respect when they give. Last, and perhaps most importantly, when we prevent or discourage the poor from giving, we may very well be robbing them of blessings the Lord has in store for them. This text shows in the most dramatic way that the woman received the blessing of her son's healing after she gave. Blessing follows obedience.

NOT GIVING AFFECTS OTHERS

We have already seen the tremendous blessing the widow received, but we need to keep in mind that her blessing relied not only on her obedience but also on Elijah's obedience. Quite possibly, she would not have received the blessing if Elijah had not also been obedient to God. Just as great blessing came because both obeyed, there is a cost to others when we do not obey the command to give.

Consider this: what would have happened to the widow if Elijah had not shown the faith and obedience to go to Sidon? What if he'd told the Lord "no" and refused to believe his needs would be cared for? Is it possible that he never would have encountered the widow and her son and been used of God to bring great blessing into their lives? Is it possible that, lacking the opportunity to test her faith and obedience, the widow might have trusted in her own strength for her family's survival and ended up starving to death after her flour and oil ran out?

I wonder how many people will not have an opportunity to hear the gospel because of the financial disobedience of Christians. How many of our neighbors will not go to Heaven because we never gave of ourselves to them in time, money, or service?

Scripture instructs us to *bear one another's burdens, and thereby fulfill the law of Christ* (Galatians 6:2), but many times some of the people we worship, fellowship, and attend weekly groups with are in great financial need, and we would never know it. There might be a young couple across the aisle from you wearing half-hearted smiles but secretly distressed about paying their monthly rent or buying groceries for their children. Maybe it's an elderly widow whose husband neglected to provide for her needs after his death. Maybe it's even your church leader, a servant of God who, like Elijah and so many others across this nation, struggles week after week to keep his or her ministries afloat so that people can hear the Gospel. What happens to these people when we do not give? What happens to the countless others they could have reached with God's Word? Does your giving of your time, money, or service help fulfill Christ's commandment to love others?

INVISIBLE BLESSINGS OF OBEDIENCE

A final lesson on giving to learn from Elijah and the widow of Zarephath is the concept of invisible blessing. There may be dire situations coming our way that never arrive because of our obedience, and this is a tremendous unseen blessing. It is hard to quantify such blessings, but acknowledging what could have happened in a given situation helps us see God's sovereignty and hand of mercy as acts of lovingkindness and blessing.

If Elijah had given in to his fear that God would not provide for him, or if the widow had given in to her fear and not given Elijah her last bit of flour, what could have happened when tragedy struck the woman's family shortly thereafter?

Now it came about after these things that the son of the woman, the mistress of the house, became sick; and his sickness was so severe that there was no breath left in him. So she said to Elijah, "What do I have to do with you, O man of God? You have come to me to bring my iniquity to remembrance and to put my son to death!" He said to her, "Give me your son." Then he took him from her bosom and carried him up to the upper room where he was living, and laid him on his own bed. And he called to the LORD and said, "O LORD my God, have You also brought calamity to the widow with whom I am staying, by causing her son to die?" Then he stretched himself upon the child three times, and called to the LORD and said, "O LORD my God, I pray You, let this child's life return to him." The LORD heard the voice of Elijah, and the life of the child returned to him and he revived. Elijah took the child and brought him down from the upper room into the house and gave him to his mother; and Elijah said, "See, your son is alive." Then the woman said to Elijah, "Now I know that you are a man of God and that the word of the LORD in your mouth is true." 1 Kings 17:17-24

The widow's story ends like most of the stories about giving. When her son dies, Elijah gives instruction from God: *Give me your son."* Then comes the test of faith: how will she respond? In verse 19, the widow gives her son's body to Elijah, proving her faith by obedience, and then blessing follows. In the widow's case, the blessing involved another dramatic example of the Lord's provision. Her son's life was restored: *The Lord heard the voice of Elijah, and the life of the child returned.*

Now, don't get me wrong: I am not suggesting that the lesson in this miraculous story is that if the Lord does not dramatically provide for your family or heal or revive a sick or dead relative that you are necessarily living in disobedience. While God can and does miraculously intervene in many circumstances, poverty, sickness, and death are often simply the tragic result of living in a fallen world. God's principles for giving bring blessing, but that does not mean our lives will be without sorrow or hardship.

WHAT ARE YOU DOING WITH YOUR RESOURCES?

On Easter Sunday 1994, a seventy-one-year-old woman named Bertha Adams died alone in her apartment in West Palm Beach, Florida. Officials investigating her death found evidence that her death was poverty-related. Not only was her home a "pigpen... the biggest mess you can imagine," but neighbors reported that she had begged food from them and had gotten the few clothes she owned from the Salvation Army. At the time of her death, Ms. Adams had wasted away to a scant fifty pounds.[21]

To their surprise, investigators later found that two keys discovered among Ms. Adams' belongings opened safe-deposit boxes at local banks. The first box contained 700 AT&T stock certificates, hundreds of other valuable certificates, bonds, solid financial securities, and a stack of cash amounting to nearly $200,000. The second box contained almost $600,000. In total the woman's estate was worth well over a million dollars, which later went to distant relatives who were just as surprised as police investigators had been at the origin of their inheritance.

This woman may be contrasted with the widow of Zarephath. The former was a millionaire who died a victim of her own inability to recognize and utilize the resources at hand. Hers was the misery of a spirit of poverty. This is how the widow of Zarephath lived at the beginning of the story, but as God transformed her life she began to realize the wealth of provision available to her when she put her trust in the Almighty.

There are a lot of God's people who have not put their trust in His Word as it concerns the financial and spiritual realms and so they are living far below

---

21 - Swindoll, C. (1994). *The Finishing Touch: Becoming God's Masterpiece*, pp. 448-449. Dallas, TX: Word

the poverty line. This is not God's plan. "Thus saith the Lord" should be enough for any of us to take Him at His word and begin to do what He has called us to do with our resources.

My prayer is that we would be an obedient people, foolish in the eyes of the world, perhaps, but wise in the ways of God. When we read God's Word, we should say, "What God says, by His grace I will do, starting now." May we "make him a little bread first" and feel the excitement of seeing God work.

GIVING BY SHARING:

THE GLEANERS AND THE EARLY CHURCH

Leviticus 19:9-10 tells us, *Now when you reap the harvest of your land, you shall not reap to the very corners of your field, nor shall you gather the gleanings of your harvest. Nor shall you glean your vineyard, nor shall you gather the fallen fruit of your vineyard; you shall leave them for the needy and for the stranger. I am the LORD your God.*

In this passage we find another valuable giving principle that seems very foreign to our American lifestyle: we are to share with others by not consuming all we produce. We are to give a small portion of what we earn to those less fortunate. Like other biblical principals, this is easy to understand but difficult to implement.

In biblical times, families did not consume all they could produce. They systematically and routinely left a remainder of the crops for those less fortunate. Farmers did not gather the crops for, cook for, or feed the poor. Those who needed food had to take responsibility to seek and harvest it for themselves.

The biblical plan is a far cry from social

programs that encourage people to think the only work they have to do is walk to the mailbox once a month to collect money to pay their bills. Such programs have their place as a temporary aid until people are more financially stable, in the same way that crutches are a temporary aid for a man recovering from an injured foot. As soon as the man is able to support his weight on his own, the crutches are put aside. Too often, however, public assistance has become a permanent crutch for those with no intention of supporting themselves and who are, in effect, social parasites.

BOAZ'S TREATMENT OF THE GLEANERS

And Ruth the Moabitess said to Naomi, "Please let me go to the field and glean among the ears of grain after one in whose sight I may find favor." And she said to her, "Go, my daughter." So she departed and went and gleaned in the field after the reapers; and she happened to come to the portion of the field belonging to Boaz, who was of the family of Elimelech.... Then Boaz said to Ruth, "Listen carefully, my daughter. Do not go to glean in another field; furthermore, do not go on from this one, but stay here with my maids. Let your eyes be on the field which they reap, and go after them. Indeed, I have commanded the servants not to touch you. When you are thirsty, go to the water jars and drink from what the servants draw." Then she fell on her face, bowing to the ground and said to him, "Why have I found favor in your sight that you should take notice of me, since I am a foreigner?" Boaz replied to her, "All that you have done for your mother-in-law after the death of your husband has been fully reported to me, and how you left your father and your mother and the land of your birth, and came to a people that you did not previously know. May the LORD reward your work, and your wages be full from the LORD, the God of Israel, under whose wings you have come to seek refuge." ...When she rose to glean, Boaz commanded his servants, saying, "Let her glean even among the sheaves, and do not insult her. Also you shall purposely pull out for her some grain from the bundles and leave it that she may glean, and do not rebuke her." So she gleaned in the field until evening. Ruth 2:2-4, 8-12, 15-17

SHARING HELPS THOSE IN NEED

God never intended His people to spend all their resources on themselves; His heart is for sharing. And yet in every community in America, there are families that live at or below the poverty level and are barely getting by. There are senior citizens who, after working all of their lives have to make a decision: purchase medicine or purchase food? I have even heard of poor senior citizens who bought meat-flavored pet food for personal consumption because traditional meat was too expensive. This is a travesty.

There are hurting and needy people everywhere we look—in our neighborhoods and communities, and whether we recognize it or not, in our local churches. For a great many of us, it would not take much of a sacrifice to help; even a few dollars could make a difference in someone else's life. What if you ate out one less time this month or cut back on a couple of $5 lattes? Can you imagine what would happen in your church if each family assisted another family in the community? I can tell you what would happen. Your church would grow. I wonder if one of the reasons that we have seen very little growth in American Christianity these last twenty years is because Christians in the U.S., by and large, are not sharing with those less fortunate.

Let us look at what it means to give up something to help others, not just from your abundance but from your sustenance as well. This takes us to Acts 2:45-46,

And they began selling their property and possessions

*and were sharing them with all, as anyone might have
need. Day by day continuing with one mind in the
temple, and breaking bread from house to house, they
were taking their meals together with gladness and
sincerity of heart.*

Re-read these verses. The Christians of the
early church were selling their possessions to help
others. Are you getting this? Giving instead of keeping,
helping instead of hoarding. This boggles the American
mind. When was the last time someone you know sold
a personal possession solely to benefit someone else?
When was the last time you sold something and gave the
proceeds to another in need? Just for the record, I point
this question at myself, too.

An interesting thing happens when we get new
clothes or furniture. We all of a sudden become very
charitable and we give our old things to Goodwill or call
the Salvation Army. When I think about the early church
and I consider how they sold property and possessions to
help others, I wonder if the way we give our possessions
away needs to be reconsidered. What if the next time
you bought new clothes or new living room furniture,
you gave your brand-new purchase to a family that has
never been able to have that experience? What a radical
application of the command *Do to others what you
would have them do to you* (Matthew 7:12, NIV)!

I do not believe this passage in Acts is saying we
should never purchase nice things for ourselves, nor do
I interpret it to mean that socialism should be a way of
life. These verses do not indicate that the early church
pooled all its resources; it simply says they were willing
to sell, sacrifice, and help if necessary. Their desire
to help each other was spontaneous and voluntary,
motivated by an understanding of God's generous love.
I believe that, like the early church, we are to hold our
possessions lightly and be willing to sell them if we feel

directed to do so by God to help meet another's need.

GIVING WITH GRATITUDE AND JOY:

THE MACEDONIAN CHURCH

Now, brethren, we wish to make known to you the grace of God which has been given in the churches of Macedonia, that in a great ordeal of affliction their abundance of joy and their deep poverty overflowed in the wealth of their liberality. For I testify that according to their ability, and beyond their ability, they gave of their own accord. 2 Corinthians 8:1-3

We should give simply because the Bible instructs us to do so. If God's Word tells us to do something, we can be sure of two things: a way has been provided for us to obey the command, and in the long run we will be better off obeying than disobeying. This concept is simple but rich in truth.

One of the benefits of our obedience to God's Word is that He will bless us, and we have seen several Scriptures that apply this principle specifically to giving. In and of itself, there really is nothing wrong with giving to receive. But in order to be long-time givers who fully understand the principles of sowing and reaping, we must also love the Lord Jesus wholeheartedly, if only because we do not know when we will reap. Scripture teaches, *We love Him, because He first loved us* (1 John 4:19, KJV). As our love for God and our faith in Him grows, especially in the area of giving, fear will be pushed away and replaced by faith because *perfect love casts out fear* (1 John 4:18).

There is much said in the Bible about rewards, so we do not want to discount the fact that we will be rewarded for being obedient to God's Word. I believe God is more concerned that we start giving and growing, developing in our giving like a baby who learns to walk amidst stumbles and falls, than He is about whether or not we have perfect motives. He can work with our hearts on our motives for giving as we go along.

GRACE GIVING

As we look at a New Testament example of giving, there does not seem to be a better word to use than grace. A close look at 2 Corinthians 8-9, where Paul addresses the topic of giving, shows us that grace is the predominant theme, mentioned six times. Consider these definitions of grace:

"The favor or kindness shown without regard to the worth or merit of the one who receives it and in spite of what the person deserves."[22]

"A favor done without expectation of return, the absolute free expression of the loving kindness of God to men."[23]

"A key attribute of God. Although the grace of God is always free and undeserved, it must never be taken for granted. Grace is only enjoyed within the COVENANT— the gift is given by God, and the gift is received by people through repentance."[24]

Under grace, we take action based on our understanding and appreciation of what God has already done, not what we want Him to do. Gone is the Old Testament idea of "if I do _____, God will do_____." He has already done His part; grace-filled giving is our response to God's work in our lives.

Paul reminds the Corinthian church of God's work of grace in 2 Corinthians 8-9. He begins by mentioning grace (2 Corinthians 8:1): *Now, brethren, we wish to make known to you the grace of God which has been given in the churches of Macedonia* and then he reminds them of the graciousness of God shown through

22 - Youngblood, R. (1995). *Nelson's New Illustrated Bible Dictionary.* Nashville, TN: Thomas Nelson.
23 - Zodhiates, S. (1992).
24 - Youngblood, R. (1995).

Jesus' sacrifice:

*So we urged Titus that as he had previously made
a beginning, so he would also complete in you this
gracious work as well. But just as you abound in
everything, in faith and utterance and knowledge and
in all earnestness and in the love we inspired in you, see
that you abound in this gracious work also. I am not
speaking this as a command, but as proving through
the earnestness of others the sincerity of your love also.
For you know the grace of our Lord Jesus Christ, that
though He was rich, yet for your sake He became poor,
so that you through His poverty might become rich.*
2 Corinthians 8:6-9

We can also view this work of grace in 2
Corinthians 8:19, NIV, *What is more, He was chosen by
the churches to accompany us as we carry the offering,
which we administer in order to honor the Lord Himself
and to show our eagerness to help,* and in 2 Corinthians
9:8, *And God is able to make all grace abound to you,
so that always having all sufficiency in everything, you
may have an abundance for every good deed.* Paul is
explaining here that when we give to Jesus and His work,
not only do we get to see grace at work but God provides
a way for us to do what His Word says.

Chapter 9 closes with, *While they also, by
prayer on your behalf, yearn for you because of the
surpassing grace of God in you. Thanks be to God for
His indescribable gift* (2 Corinthians 9:14-15)! This
shows us that our giving is a reflection of the grace we
have chosen to receive, and God certainly has given us an
ample amount. When we stop and reflect on all God has
done for us, it becomes easy to be giving Christians.

GRATITUDE IN GIVING LIKE THE MACEDONIANS

When we give with an attitude of appreciation,
several things occur, we become consistent in our giving,

we plan our giving and, we become spontaneous in our giving. In our appreciation for what Jesus has done, we will be giving at least a tenth of our resources to the church, but we will not get stuck in the 10% rut, giving only a tenth out of habit. In the tundra of Alaska there is a saying: "Be careful which rut your car goes into, because you will be in it for the next twenty miles." An attitude of appreciation frees up the supply line from God to us and back again and keeps us from getting stuck in a habit.

When we give out of appreciation, a threefold blessing occurs. Paul addresses this in the conclusion of his letter to the Philippians: *But I have received everything in full and have an abundance; I am amply supplied, having received from Epaphroditus what you have sent, a fragrant aroma, an acceptable sacrifice, well-pleasing to God* (4:18). Paul has caught the attitude of gratitude. He says to the Philippians, "I'm full." Think for a moment how it feels after finishing a good meal in which you have eaten just enough food. Paul is saying, "Hey guys, I feel good. Not only am I full, but I'm appreciative of what you've done."

Giving brings a blessing of abundance to the receiver. Paul acknowledges that not only is he full, he has abundance. Clearly, here in God-blessed America we have abundance. Did you have to decide what to wear today? Did you have to decide what to eat? Have you seen or rented a movie in the last thirty days? Do you have a television? Abundance is not our problem; our problem is we have to develop our attitude of appreciation.

Giving brings pleasure to God (Philippians 4:18). Without an attitude of appreciation, the Philippians never would have given to Paul. Paul mentions that no other people helped him (Philippians 4:15).

Giving brings blessing to the giver. Paul says,

Not that I seek the gift itself, but I seek for the profit
which increases to your account (Philippians 4:17).

THE ROLE OF JOY IN GIVING

This type of giving involves gladness, which
has also been interpreted as "cheer, cheerfulness,
good or high spirits, joy, delight, pleasure, happiness,
felicity, jubilation, exhilaration, glee, elation; joviality,
merriment, jollity, mirth, mirthfulness, hilarity."[25] Are
these the words that describe the attitude in your church
when the offering plates are passed? Let me ask you
an even more personal question: do the above words
describe the attitude in your heart towards the offering?

New Testament giving is seasoned with joy. In 2
Corinthians 8-9, we see the theme of gladness as Paul so
beautifully lays out the text for us:

And now, brothers, we want you to know about the
grace that God has given the Macedonian churches.
Out of the most severe trial, their overflowing joy and
their extreme poverty welled up in rich generosity. For
I testify that they gave as much as they were able, and
even beyond their ability. 2 Corinthians 8:1-3

The Macedonians gave out of deep poverty.
Certainly all of us have hard times on our journey
through life, perhaps even seasons of want or times
during which there were things we desired to purchase
but did not have the resources to do so. This does not
mean we have experienced poverty. The Macedonians,
on the other hand, really did know poverty. Despite
their scarcity, their attitude was one of joy; they wanted
to participate in giving. What then should our attitude
toward giving be?

In most cases, our primary giving should
be through the local church. Having said that, I
acknowledge that when we give to the local church we

---

25 - Rodale, J.I., Urdang, L., & Laroche, N. (1978). *The Synonym Finder.*
Emmaus, PA: Rodale Press.

benefit, and this is good. For one thing, any ministry you or your family receives from the local church is a benefit you derive from your giving. Certainly if you and other families did not give to your church, your church would cease to exist. So there is absolutely nothing wrong with receiving some benefit from your giving.

In the particular case of the Macedonian Christians, neither they nor their organization were going to be the direct beneficiaries of the money they were giving; the funds were going to be used for the church in Jerusalem to help people that, in all likelihood, they would never meet. They nonetheless sacrificed deeply with great joy. Think about your church's last building campaign. Remember how hard it was to raise all of the money needed? How much harder it would have been to raise the money if it was intended for a church in a different country?

In 2 Corinthians 9:7, NIV Paul writes, *Each one must do just as he has purposed in his heart, not grudgingly or under compulsion, for God loves a cheerful giver.* You may have heard that we get the word "hilarious" from the Greek word hilaros, which is translated as "cheerful" in the New Testament. If you're like me, you've wondered if this means we are to be "hilarious" givers, and if so, what exactly that looks like. Should we be cracking jokes and laughing while we put our money in the collection plate? How strange we would look to unbelievers who visited our worship services!

Zodhiates points out that hilaros actually "denotes a happy, glad or cheerful state of mind and not one overcome with laughter or mirth, or one humorously affected."[26] Thus interpreted, we see, we see that Paul is concerned that we make the connection between being giving people and being joyful people. It is possible to be a person who gives but does not for one reason or another experience all the joy God has in store. On the

---

26 - Zodhiates, S. (1992).

other hand, it is impossible to experience all the joy God has for you and yet be a person that does not give to God's work.

THE REWARDS OF GIVING LIKE THE MACEDONIANS

Some teach only the rewards of giving. Christians who are busy adjusting their halos and being concerned with their end reward can sometimes construe this as a sort of prosperity gospel. Though this is false theology, it is true that just as there are negative consequences for being disobedient to God's Word, there are also positive consequences for being obedient. Obedience yields rewards in other areas of life, so why should it be any different in the area of finances?

Generous, joyful Christians do reap rewards. In our text, Paul refers to the reward of abundance. The original language can be defined this way: "increase, abound, overflow, excel, exceed, have plenty, have more than enough to provide an abundance."[27] Abundance is used six times in 2 Corinthians 8-9 to speak of the the overflowing joy, the wealth of liberality, and the promise of reaping bountifully. 2 Corinthians 9:6 tells us that the abundance available to us is determined by how we sow and reap: *Now this I say, he who sows sparingly will also reap sparingly; and he who sows bountifully will also reap bountifully.* Just two verses later we see the connection between giving and God's provision made again: *And God is able to make all grace abound to you, so that always having all sufficiency in everything, you may have an abundance for every good deed* (2 Corinthians 9:8). We have abundance in this time of grace to accomplish every good thing we set out to do. Finally, in verse 11 we see an abundance of thanksgiving available to us: *You will be enriched in everything for all liberality, which through us is producing thanksgiving to God.*

---

27 - ibid

I don't know about you, but I am extremely interested in experiencing all these things in my life. Jesus has already accomplished this for us. It is available now. The more we participate in God's way of doing things and invest in the things that interest God, the more we will experience the abundance waiting for us.

GIVING AS AN ACT OF WORSHIP

MARY'S GENEROSITY

Mary was one of three siblings who were close friends with Jesus. Jesus stayed at their house. He ate with them. He taught them. He brought Mary's brother Lazarus back from the dead. But though all three loved Him and He loved them, there was something special about Mary. Jesus recognized in her a rare depth of spiritual understanding. He commended her for understanding what was truly important in this life: worshipping God.

The setting of this story is one of extremes. Lazarus has just been brought back from the dead, so it is a time of celebration. As word spreads of this newest miracle, opposition begins to mount. Jesus goes into the desert and then travels from there to Jerusalem. The air is thick with hostility as the time of His arrest and execution fast approaches, though it seems only Jesus and Mary have a foreboding sense of what is about to happen. It is then that Mary makes a decision that caused confusion and consternation in some onlookers, but it was a decision that could have only been motivated by love for Jesus. In this act, she provided a great example of the essential principles behind giving as an act of worship.

WORSHIPFUL GIVING IS COSTLY

Mary therefore took a pound of very costly perfume of

pure nard, and anointed the feet of Jesus and wiped His feet with her hair; and the house was filled with the fragrance of the perfume. But Judas Iscariot, one of His disciples, who was intending to betray him, said, "Why was this perfume not sold for three hundred denarii and given to the poor?" Now he said this, not because he cared about poor people, but because he was a thief, and as he had the money box he used to pilfer what was put into it. Therefore Jesus said, "Let her alone, so that she may keep it for the day of my burial. For you always have the poor with you, but you do not always have Me." John 12:3-8

We learn an important lesson from Mary's example: when we give to God, our gift should cost us something. We are told Mary's gift was nard, a rare and costly perfume that cost three hundred denarii. In Matthew 20:2, we learn that a denarius was equal to a day's wage. A little simple math shows that Mary's gift to Jesus added up to almost a year's wages. It has been theorized that her reason for having such a costly item in the house was because she had purchased it to help prepare her brother's body for burial. Remember that until shortly before the incident recorded here, Lazarus had been dead and entombed. But Mary did not use this expensive perfume on her dead brother; instead, she used it on the living Jesus.

This amazes me. I do not know anyone who would offer such an extravagant gift. Mary practiced the first and greatest commandment by worshiping and loving Jesus with her whole heart and soul. Her gift was special to Jesus because it was special to her.

Judas, in contrast, shows us a heart unable to worship or love. Bound up in his own greed, he pretends to appear spiritual. He says, *Why was this perfume not sold for three hundred denarii and given to poor people?* (John 12:5) Judas sounds prudent, but his motive was evil; his is not the example we are to follow.

HAPPENS AT THE FEET OF JESUS

Mary's heart to worship Jesus was evidenced not only by her gift but also by her physical position in relation to Jesus. Mary is at center stage three times in the Bible, and each time she is recorded as being at the feet of Jesus, worshiping Him. In Luke 10:39 she sits at His feet to hear His words in John 11:32 she is at His feet kneeling in sorrow over the death of her brother and in John 12:3-8 she worships as she gives. You get the idea from this pattern that Mary lived her life in a wonderful place—at the feet of Jesus.

I believe it is possible, for a while, to fake being at the feet of Jesus. When however, you see a person at the feet of Jesus giving the equivalent of a year's salary, you can be sure this person truly worships Him. By worship, I am not speaking of singing praise songs to Him as we do today in our church services. Mary worshiped Jesus with her life.

AIMS TO PLEASE GOD RATHER THAN MAN

In the first verse of this text, John 12:3, Mary wipes Jesus' feet with her hair. This is significant because any woman who would let down her hair in public was thought to be immoral. In the parallel passage of Mark 14:3-9 the crowd's reaction to this act is quite telling. Many were indignant and turned on her in fury, scolding and reproving her, criticizing her sharply, deeply offended by her act of worship. Yet, I see nowhere in the text that Mary paid any attention to these critics. She just wanted to worship Jesus. She was not intimidated by what others might have thought of her but was secure in His love.

Security prompts surrender. Compare Mary's security to our attitude when we give something significant to the Lord. We tend to want to appear moral, pious, or righteous. But Mary gave all she could, even in the face of severe criticism.

DOES NOT HESITATE BUT GIVES NOW

Scripture tells us that after Jesus' death, other women came to anoint His body, but when they arrived to do so it was already gone. Imagine what they must have thought. They wanted to give, but they chose to wait. Their waiting left them wanting. From Mary's example we learn that the time to give is always now.

A line from an oft-quoted C. T. Studd poem reads, "Only one life 'twill soon be past/ Only what's done for Christ will last." When I hear this line I think of a story I once heard about an elderly couple, an 80-year-old bride and her 81-year-old bridegroom, that hobbled down the aisle to be married after dating for fifty years. When the preacher asked why they had waited so long to get married, the groom replied, "We wanted to wait until we could afford it."

This story reminds me to avoid the example of many well-meaning Christians who think, "We want to give, but first we want to save up for a house," or "We'll give after we make that first mortgage payment/ purchase the new furniture," or "Oh, we definitely plan on giving... just as soon as we have children/mom goes back to work/the kids are out of private school/we get these weddings paid for..." Almost before we know it our lives will have passed us by, and we will have never gotten into the habit of giving consistently to Jesus.

The reality is that there never will be a time to "afford" giving to Jesus. We will be in for a huge disappointment when we get to heaven and tell the Lord, "Really, we wanted to give...we were just waiting for the right time." Like Mary, we need to give now. Ask the Lord what He would have you give.

HAS A LASTING IMPACT ON OTHERS

One gets the impression Mary's house was of good size. For one thing, she was able to entertain a crowd of people. For another, she had expensive perfume on hand. At the very least, the perfume could have been her dowry. Giving it away might have dashed all hopes of a potential husband. We read in John 12:3 that after the bottle had been broken and the perfume used on Jesus, the smell pervaded the entire house. In the future, no doubt whenever people who were there smelled nard; they must have been brought immediately back to the scene with vivid clarity. Mary's lavish gift was significant and striking. No one could miss its lingering impact.

Maybe as you just read this you thought to yourself, "Oh sure, if I had a large house, and if I could afford a bottle of perfume worth a year's salary, I'd give generously to Jesus too." This is only true if you are giving generously to Jesus with what you already have. Wealth does not bring generosity; rather, a person with a generous character will be a generous giver whether he is wealthy or poor (Ecclesiastes 5:10-11, Luke 16:10). Mary's example also teaches us that you will not be remembered or held accountable for what you cannot do, only for what you can do. You may not have the means to give like Mary did, but you can certainly give from what you do have. For what will you be remembered?

PLEASES GOD

We all have a desire to make an impact and to be remembered as someone who mattered. Yet most of us will only be remembered by a few family members and friends. Anybody who becomes familiar with the gospel hears the story of Mary. Her example shows that giving is not only sanctioned by Jesus but it also pleases Him. When Judas rebukes Mary for her action, Jesus tells him to *let her alone, so that she may keep it for the day of My burial* (John 12:7). And Jesus' approval is the only one that truly matters.

In his book, *The Man in the Mirror*, Patrick Morley asks the following questions:

Can you name the ten wealthiest men in the world?

Can you name the ten most admired men in America?

Can you name the top ten corporate executives in America?

Can you name the last ten presidents of the United States?

Can you name the last ten Nobel Prize winners?[28]

No matter how high we climb in popularity or importance, most of us will not be remembered. Mary shows us a way to be remembered—give to Jesus. Arno Clemens Gaebelein[29] points this out in his commentary on the Gospel of Matthew:

"Mary's act has come down to us, in the gospel record, coupled with His blessed name. No one can read the Gospel without reading also the memorial of her personal devotion. Empires have risen, flourished, and passed away into the region of silence and oblivion. Monuments have been erected to commemorate human genius, greatness, and philanthropy—and these monuments have crumbled into dust, but the act of this woman still lives, and shall live forever. The hand of the Master has erected a monument to her, which shall never, no never, perish. May we have grace to imitate her, and, in this day, when there is so much of human effort in the way of philanthropy, may our works, whatever they are, be the fruit of our hearts' appreciation of an absent, rejected, crucified Lord!"

Truly, Mary has a monument in her name that will never go away. In Matthew 26 we read, *Truly I say to you, wherever this gospel is preached in the whole*

28 - Morley, P. (1989). *The Man in the Mirror: Seeking the 24 Problems Men Face.* Grand Rapids, MI: Zondervan.
29 - Gaebelein, A.C. (1910). *The Gospel of Matthew: An Exposition.* New York: Our Hope.

world, what this woman has done shall also be spoken of in memory of her.

The Bible clearly tells us that giving is an act of worship, plain and simple. If our income belongs entirely to the Lord and we spend the portion He calls us to give on something other than His work, does that make us more like the generous Mary or the thieving Judas? What memorials are your spending habits writing about you?

Chapter 8

HOW NOT TO GIVE:
PATTERNS IN THE BIBLE

What differences do you
see between Judas' giving
and yours?

Do you struggle with
wanting to give only for the
approval of others? If so,
how can you change this
desire?

Have you ever given
purposely to protect your
heart from greed or an
unhealthy clinging to
material things?

Judas' money-loving character can teach us a lot about what not to do when it comes to giving.

Just as there are powerful examples throughout the Bible of those who sacrificed much to give and were blessed accordingly, there are also many examples of those whose approach to giving serves as a warning to us. Although the lessons learned in each example are specific, there is one common failing in all: the sin of pride, or the attitude that giving is about us rather than the One from whom all good things in our lives have come.

We sometimes become proud of ourselves for giving. I think this temptation is strongest when we first begin to give or when we grow beyond a basic percentage of giving to areas of consistent, liberal giving. The story of David and the fundraising for the temple helps us remember that when we give, we are doing nothing more than returning to God what was, what is, and what will forever remain His. Lest we become puffed up, the following humble prayer of David's stands in contrast to our supposed generosity:

Yours, O LORD, is the greatness and the power and the glory and the victory and the majesty, indeed everything that is in the heavens and the earth; Yours is the dominion, O LORD, and You exalt Yourself as head over all. Both riches and honor come from You, and You rule over all, and in Your hand is power and might; and it lies in Your hand to make great, and to strengthen everyone. Now therefore, our God we thank You, and praise Your glorious name. But who am I and who are my people that we should be able to offer as generously as this? For all things come from You, and from Your hand we have given You. 1 Chronicles 29:11-14

The cure for pride when we give (no matter our level of giving) is to remember the simple fact found in verse 12: Both riches and honor come from You. In our self-sufficient, technological world, it is good to remember all good things come from the Lord (James 1:17). Paul states this in an equally powerful way: *For from Him and through Him and to Him are all things. To Him be the glory* (Romans 11:36).

Christians in agrarian societies do not have a problem with this concept. They understand that on their own they do not have the power to make any crop thrive. What if you imagined yourself at that level for a minute? Let's say you genetically produce a seed—a hybrid—of your own design. You plant it and somehow are able to control the weather so it's not too hot or too cold for the seed to germinate, grow, and multiply. You might be able to control some of these things on a small scale, maybe in a greenhouse. But to produce enough to feed the country, or even the world, you would need the Lord's cooperation.

David understood this: *Now therefore, our God, we thank You, and praise Your glorious name* (1 Chronicles 29:13). The result of our giving is not supposed to be pride. It is supposed to be a healthy, thankful recognition of who God is and why we are given our next breath.

We need to grasp the concept of who really owns what. In Psalm 50:10, the psalmist tells of God's ownership of all creation: *For every beast of the forest is Mine, the cattle on a thousand hills.* I know a pastor who is fond of saying, "God not only owns the animals and the hills, but He owns the seed, He owns the water, and He owns the grass on the hills that the cattle eat."

Keeping God's ownership as the primary focus of fundraising for a large project will keep us from pride and help us be more thankful in our giving: *Whatever you do in Word or deed, do all in the name of the Lord Jesus, giving thanks through Him to God the Father* (Colossians 3:17).

THE JUDAS SYNDROME

Judas' name means "Let God be praised," yet it has come to stand for betrayal of all that is good: greed, treachery, disloyalty, and failure. The name is used today to designate the goat that leads sheep to the slaughterhouse, and in the Far East it is the name for a type of plant that looks sweet but is bitter to the taste.[30]

In the New Testament Judas was a follower of Christ, but not only did he sell Jesus out for thirty pieces of silver, he sold himself out as well and paid for his greed with his life. His money-loving character can teach us a lot about what not to do when it comes to giving.

DECEITFULNESS

Jesus, therefore, six days before the Passover, came to Bethany where Lazarus was, whom Jesus had raised from the dead. So they made Him a supper there, and Martha was serving; but Lazarus was one of those reclining at the table with Him. Mary then took a pound of very costly perfume of pure nard, and anointed the feet of Jesus and wiped His feet with her hair; and the house was filled with the fragrance of the perfume. But Judas Iscariot, one of His disciples, who was intending to betray Him, said, "Why was this perfume not sold for three hundred denarii and given to poor people?" Now he said this, not because he was concerned about

---

30 - Merriam-Webster, Inc. (2008). *Merriam-Webster's Collegiate Dictionary (11th ed.)*

*the poor, but because he was a thief, and as he had
the money box, he used to pilfer what was put into it.*
John 12:1-6

From outward appearances, Judas' comment
seems genuine and understandable. We do not know
much about Judas, but he must have shown himself to
have decent money-management skills because Jesus
and the disciples had chosen him to be in charge of the
coin purse. He had his cover down so well that even
when Jesus told the disciples in the upper room that one
of them would betray Him and Judas asked, "Is it I?" the
rest of the disciples did not suspect him as the traitor.

In the first film of the *Pirates of the Caribbean*
series, a British ship is under attack by ghost-pirates, and
out of fear and cowardice the governor hides in a cabin
to save himself. Later, when the pirates are vanquished,
he emerges like a modern politician, glad-handling the
survivors with a thumbs-up, "We did it!" attitude. Judas'
hypocrisy in the passage above is just as obvious—or
at least it was to God, who recorded this example for
generations of readers to come. Judas wanted others to
think he was better than he was, but he was exposed for
his true self: a greedy grabber.

DISPARAGING WORDS

Judas belittled Mary by his comments. He
described her loving and generous gift as a frivolous,
wasteful gesture. His words colored others' convictions
as well, affecting the other disciples to such an extent
that they also chimed in to belittle Mary's actions: *But
some were indignantly remarking to one another, "Why
has this perfume been wasted? For this perfume might
have been sold for over three hundred denarii, and the
money given to the poor." And they were scolding her*
(Mark 14:4-5).

Godly givers should bless sacrificial giving to

the kingdom of God, not curse it. Whenever there is a financial need in the church, it is important to watch our words when speaking about the need or church leaders' response. We must avoid negative and disparaging words like Judas' that would cause our brothers and sisters in Christ to stumble or be discouraged from giving. Wouldn't such criticism discourage you from giving?

DISREPUTABLE CONDUCT

In this passage we see that Judas *said this, not because he was concerned about the poor* (John 12:6a). Judas had no compassion for or interest in helping the poor people he was speaking of; rather, *he was a thief, and as he had the money box, he used to pilfer what was put into it* (John 12:6b).

Good magicians and charlatans use sleight-of-hand distraction to get their victims and audiences to look one way while they do something in another direction. Judas realized if he could get people focused on Mary and what she was doing, they would not notice what he was doing. He pilfered and embezzled, not as a one-time act of weakness but habitually, until his conduct became his character and his character became his condemnation.

DOOMED CHARACTER

Judas was distracted by his covetousness and his desire for power and prestige. Disillusioned because Jesus said His kingdom was to be spiritual and not physical or material, Judas thought he would cut his losses or force Jesus' hand, and in doing so he sealed his fate:

During supper, the devil having already put into the heart of Judas Iscariot, the son of Simon, to betray Him...So when He had dipped the morsel, He took

and gave it to Judas, the son of Simon Iscariot. After
the morsel, Satan then entered into him. Therefore
Jesus said to him, "What you do, do quickly" ...So after
receiving the morsel, he [Judas] went out immediately.
John 13:2, 26-27, 30

Notice that it was in the spiritual setting of
the Last Supper that Judas really began to listen to the
whispers of the enemy and entertain his dark thoughts.
Satan tempts us with greed and covetousness, hoping it
will overtake us.

DIRE CONSEQUENCES

Then when Judas, who had betrayed Him, saw that
He had been condemned, he felt remorse and returned
the thirty pieces of silver to the chief priests and elders,
saying, "I have sinned by betraying innocent blood." But
they said, "What is that to us? See to that yourself!"'And
he threw the pieces of silver into the temple sanctuary
and departed; and he went away and hanged himself.
Matthew 27:3-5

Whenever we sell out God's kingdom for the
world's fare, we will be disappointed. Judas could not
take back the ungodly actions that earned him unholy
money. He reaped dire consequences. If we get money
in a dishonest way, we will not be able to enjoy it. Just
as the chief priests and elders did not care about Judas'
remorse, those who help us to get money in an ungodly
manner will not care what happens to us. Nothing is
worse than guilt from missed opportunities. In the end,
the Judas syndrome will only get in the way of giving and
make you miserable. Guard against it.

ANANIAS & SAPPHIRA

But a man named Ananias, with his wife Sapphira, sold
a piece of property, and kept back some of the price for
himself, with his wife's full knowledge, and bringing

a portion of it, he laid it at the apostles' feet. But Peter said, "Ananias, why has Satan filled your heart to lie to the Holy Spirit, and to keep back some of the price of the land? While it remained unsold, did it not remain your own? And after it was sold, was it not under your control? Why is it that you have conceived this deed in your heart? You have not lied to men, but to God." And as he heard these words, Ananias fell down and breathed his last; and great fear came over all who heard of it. The young men got up and covered him up, and after carrying him out, they buried him. Now there elapsed an interval of about three hours, and his wife came in, not knowing what had happened. And Peter responded to her, "Tell me whether you sold the land for such and such a price?" And she said, "Yes, that was the price." Then Peter said to her, "Why is it that you have agreed together to put the Spirit of the Lord to the test? Behold, the feet of those who have buried your husband are at the door, and they will carry you out as well." And immediately she fell at his feet and breathed her last, and the young men came in and found her dead, and they carried her out and buried her beside her husband. And great fear came over the whole church, and upon all who heard of these things. Acts 5:1-11

On the slope of Long's Peak in Colorado lie the ruins of a giant tree that stood for over four hundred years. Forest rangers said it had been struck by lightning fourteen times and countless storms had broken over it. After withstanding the worst of nature's blows, what finally caused the mighty tree's downfall? A tiny beetle.

This is a picture of how the sin of greed can bring us down. Some people can withstand giant temptations, but they yield time and time again to the insidious little beetle sin of greed. Greed is a termite of the soul, it will eat away any effectiveness in giving.[31]

To help us fully understand the devastating

---

31 - Vigeveno, H.S. (1970). *Sinners Anonymous.* Waco, TX: Word Books.

impact greed can have on our giving, Scripture provides the example of Ananias and his wife Sapphira, first-century followers of Christ whose self-serving attitudes incurred God's judgment and earned them a spot in the Bible for us to see ways not to give.

DESIRING DISTINCTION

Acts tells us that as the early Church began to take shape, the brethren's fundamental values of giving and sharing were obvious. There was unity and *all things were common property to them* (Acts 4:32). They were sensitive to each other's needs and were quick to share resources. Landowners and homeowners were selling personal property and donating the proceeds to the apostles for management and distribution to the needy as the leadership saw fit. One of these Christians, a Levite named Barnabas, sold a parcel of land and presented the money to the apostles. Immediately following his gift, Ananias and Sapphira came forward. They, too, had owned some property and sold it. They came forward and publicly gave the proceeds to the apostles.

There was a radical difference between Barnabas' gift and theirs. Ananias and Sapphira lied about the profit they made from the sale so they could keep some of the money for themselves. We are not told in Scripture why they felt the need to lie; perhaps they did it to gain recognition from others. Maybe they had seen the accolades and recognition Barnabas received and wanted to keep up with the Joneses. In the Sermon on the Mount, Jesus warns: *Beware of practicing your righteousness before men to be noticed by them; otherwise you have no reward with your Father who is in heaven* (Matthew 6:1). Those who give in order to gain earthly distinction have already received all the recognition they will ever get. Unlike Barnabas, who humbly gave all the money from the sale of his property,

Ananias and Sapphira gave only enough to be noticed and admired by others.

DELIBERATE DECEPTION

The fact that Ananias and Sapphira made a sizable, voluntary donation to the church is not the point. God is not impressed by big donors. He cares more about what is in the heart than what is put in the offering plate. What was in this couple's hearts was premeditated deception. They were in collusion and had to confer beforehand to get their stories straight. They thought no one would know of their scheme, but they were wrong. We are warned in Proverbs that *The eyes of the LORD are in every place, watching the evil and the good* (15:3), and *the ways of a man are before the eyes of the LORD, and He watches all his paths* (5:21).

It seems incredible that this couple or anyone could cheat God and members of their own spiritual family, but I bet it happens much more easily than we think. I bet it began with just a simple thought that "It's our property. It's nobody's business how much we sold it for." The problem with this plan was Ananias and Sapphira forgot about God. We may be able to deceive others for a time, but we can never deceive God.

DISGUISED DISCIPLESHIP

Keep in mind that this couple's sin was not in not giving all the proceeds from the sale of their property. God would not have been angry if Ananias and Sapphira had owned up to the fact that their faith was not as strong as Barnabas' and that they were giving a portion to the church and keeping the rest. God gives us freedom to buy and sell things and give money to causes that touch our hearts. Notice what Peter says to Ananias: *While it remained unsold, did it not remain your own?*

And after it was sold, was it not under your control?
(Acts 5:4)

Ananias and Sapphira were judged and found
wanting, not because they gave too little but because
they gave a little and tried to make it look like they
gave a lot. They lied; they were hypocrites. Merriam-
Webster defines hypocrite as "a person who pretends to
be what he or she is not, who pretends to be better, but
really isn't so."[32] In Greece, a hypocrite was someone
who spoke from behind a mask that hid his or her true
identity. The word also refers to a pot that hides cracks
and blemishes with a layer of colored wax. The "hidden
hypocrite" goes undetected until either heat melts the
wax and reveals the crack or the pot is held up to the
light and the blemish becomes visible.

Rev. Henry Ward Beecher, a famous 19th
century American preacher, once wrote:

"To be a true Christian is a constant joy. To
seem to be one when we are not is to wear a hateful
yoke of bondage. In order to keep up appearances, an
insincere professor is obliged to do many things, which
are distasteful and even loathsome. He must utter many
solemn falsehoods which stick in his throat. He must
forfeit all self-respect. He lives in a constant fear that his
mask will slip and reveal his true character. Oh what a
wretched life is led by him who is trying to keep afloat
before his fellow creatures, and is constantly trying to
plug up those fatal leaks which he knows are sending
him to the bottom of the lake."[33]

We all know what it is to see or be guilty of
the hypocrisy of which Rev. Beecher spoke. A friend of
mine who worked as a youth advisor for his church was
confronted with his hypocrisy when he tried to fit in
with friends who did not live according to the principles
he taught his youth group. On one occasion, he invited
some of his youth group to an outing where his old

---

32 - Merriam-Webster, Inc. (2008).
33 - Beecher, W.C., Scoville, S., & Beecher, H.W. (2010). *A Biography of Rev. Henry Ward Beecher.* Whitefish, MT: Kessinger.

college buddies were drinking and distributing alcoholic beverages to those who were probably not of legal age. No one seemed to think anything was wrong with having alcohol at a gathering where teenagers would be present, but later one of the teens told my friend, "I always looked up to you as someone who walked closely with the Lord. When I saw what was happening, I knew you would do the right thing. I can't tell you how hurt, disappointed, and confused I was when you didn't say anything but went along with everyone else." My friend asked the younger believer for forgiveness and made a vow to be more authentic from that point on in his life.

Although many of us may never be confronted with our own hypocrisy like my friend was, ultimately, it is to God that we lie. Against Him is our sin, and it is to Him that we will answer.

DEMONIC DESIGN

Peter was grieved when he recognized how far off God's mark Ananias and Sapphira were in their twisted conception of giving. He lamented, *Ananias, why has Satan filled your heart to lie to the Holy Spirit?* (Acts 5:3). Peter discerned correctly that their action was prompted by the devil. Satan can prompt people to give in the wrong way or give to the wrong causes. Peter could see that though this couple believed they were in control of their money (while pretending God was in control), it was really Satan who was in charge. In John 8:44, Satan is called the *father of lies*, and his lies convinced Ananias and Sapphira that they could appear holy by making people think they were giving all their money and still keep a tidy nest egg to enjoy for themselves. They paid for this demonic design with their lives.

DIVINE DISPLEASURE

Notice how their sin affected God. Peter says

to them, *You have not lied to men, but to God* (Acts 5:4). The couple's sin was not against the church or the brethren. It was directly against God, and it immediately brought down His wrath. From the beginning of the early church, God was swift to deal with sin, for He knew that *a little leaven leavens the whole lump of dough* (1 Corinthians 5:6). This, of course, was not what the couple had expected. They expected fame, but instead they got a double funeral.

One of my friends once forgot to remove a dark blue pen from her jeans pocket before putting them into the laundry. As the heat increased in her brand new clothes dryer and things tumbled around, anything that came in contact with the pen was ruined. Despite a great deal of scrubbing, the stains on the clothes were permanent. In a similar manner, the sins of vanity, greed, and deception stain our giving. Had Ananias and Sapphira's sins been allowed to continue unchecked, the church would have been permanently stained and it would not have had the worldwide impact God designed it to have.

After God's swift punishment of Ananias and Sapphira, *great fear came upon the whole church, and over all who heard of these things* (Acts 5:11). There was no mistaking the lesson learned: *The fear of the Lord prolongs life, but the years of the wicked will be shortened* (Proverbs 10:27). God may not physically strike us dead, but when we pretend to be something we are not, we enter into a type of spiritual death and separation from the flow of God's presence and power. Much like breath leaving a dying body, life is drained from any ministry we touch. God hates hypocrisy; He wants believers to be the genuine article.

In Acts chapters 4-5, two types of givers are held up for our instruction. Barnabas gave in humility and honesty, and his motive was to bless others. He had a godly, giving attitude that brought joy to the body of Christ. In contrast, Ananias and Sapphira's giving serves as a cautionary tale that in our giving, we must not seek others' approval or lie, scheme, or hoard. We must not pretend to be godly, obedient, and generous disciples when we are anything but. We must not succumb to Satan's control. What must we do instead? We must give in such a way as to please God, to garner His divine pleasure, not earn His wrath. With God's help, we can be more like Barnabas, the godly giver, and less like Ananias and Sapphira, the miserly hypocrites.

Chapter 9

OVERCOMING OBSTACLES

What will it take for you to open up so you can give freely and pour blessings into others' lives?

How would you describe the measure with which you give?

What great reward would you like to receive in good measure, pressed down, shaken together, and running over into your lap from God?

Outward circumstances said one thing, but spiritual reality said something different.

Too many people gaze obsessively at their financial problems and only glance distractedly at God's solutions. Instead, we should gaze at God and glance at our problems. When God promised Abraham he would have descendants that outnumbered the stars, Abraham was an old man, and his wife Sarah was no spring chicken either. Abraham could have focused on his problems but Scripture tells us:

Without becoming weak in faith he contemplated his own body, now as good as dead since he was about a hundred years old, and the deadness of Sarah's womb; yet, with respect to the promise of God, he did not waver in unbelief but grew strong in faith, giving glory to God, and being fully assured that what God had promised, He was able also to perform. Romans 4:19-21

Outward circumstances said one thing, but spiritual reality said something different. Abraham grew strong in faith as he focused on the promises of God rather than on his own perceived limitations or fear of failure.

FIGHT FOR FINANCIAL FAITH

Just knowing that God wants to bless and

prosper those who give obediently to Him does not
necessarily make prosperity happen immediately.
Any step of faith or spiritual advancement is a fight.
Changing your financial mindset is a battle of the fiercest
kind imaginable. The serpent tried to get Eve to question
God's goodness and provision. He challenged her belief:
Indeed, has God said...? (Genesis 3:1). Naysayers can
put a damper on our financial faith by scoffing, *Can God
provide a table in the wilderness?* (Psalm 78:19).

At our worst moments we can be carnal and
unbelieving, and God knows His people question
whether following Him is really worth the trouble: *You
have said, "It is vain to serve God; and what profit
is it that we have kept His charge?"* (Malachi 3:14).
Friend, financial faith is a spiritual fight. Scripture
teaches us, *For though we walk in the flesh, we do not
war according to the flesh, for the weapons of our
warfare are not of the flesh, but divinely powerful
for the destruction of fortresses. We are destroying
speculations and every lofty thing raised up against
the knowledge of God, and we are taking every thought
captive to the obedience of Christ* (2 Corinthians 10:3-5).

Spiritual warfare means taking an aggressive
stand against the lies of Satan. We need to ban thoughts
like, "I guess I'll never have much money," "It's a sin
to have money," or "I'll always be in debt" and instead
focus on being obedient to Christ. If you are obedient in
giving tithes, offerings, and alms, you will realize those
thoughts are lies from the pit of Hell. Reject them. Satan
wants to keep uninformed Christians in bondage to a
spirit of poverty so as to cut off the supply of money
flowing into God's kingdom.

God has promised to financially bless obedient
Christians, but we must fight for what is ours. God
promised Joshua, *Every place on which the sole of your
foot treads, I have given it to you"* (Joshua 1:3), but

Joshua himself had to go claim what was his by promise. Remember, battle often precedes blessing.

GOD'S GOODNESS AND YOUR TRUST IN HIM

Therefore I urge you, brethren, by the mercies of God, to present your bodies a living and holy sacrifice, acceptable to God, which is your spiritual service of worship. Romans 12:1

As you grow in recognizing the mercies of God, you will want to submit yourself and your possessions to God. You only give to someone you trust. As you grow in trust, you will grow in giving. The guarantee for your return on investment is that God will receive your gifts as holy and acceptable. He will receive your gifts as worship.

RESPOND IN GRATITUDE

1 Chronicles 29 details David's prayer of thanksgiving and praise after God's provision of funds for the rebuilding of His temple. Consider the gratitude that overflows from David's heart:

So David blessed the Lord in the sight of all the assembly; and David said, "Blessed are You, O Lord God of Israel our father, forever and ever. Yours, O Lord, is the greatness and the power and the glory and the victory and the majesty, indeed everything that is in the heavens and the earth; Yours is the dominion, O Lord, and You exalt Yourself as head over all. Both riches and honor come from You, and You rule over all, and in Your hand is power and might; and it lies in Your hand to make great and to strengthen everyone. Now therefore, our God, we thank You, and praise Your glorious name.

"But who am I and who are my people that we should be able to offer as generously as this? For all things come from You, and from Your hand we have given You. 1 Chronicles 29:10-14

If you wish to reciprocate God's goodness and generosity, then respond out of an attitude of gratitude for all He has done for you. God's guarantee in relationship is multifaceted: He promises to be your God, to be sovereign over your life, to strengthen you, and to provide riches, honor, power, and might as you have need.

REORDER YOUR PRIORITIES

If your finances are in disarray, God promises to bring order back into your life. Submit the management of your resources to His principles. Before you can give rightly, your attitude and priorities must be made right. Sometimes this means planning and implementing a budget. Maybe you will need to reorder your spending. Transformed thinking results in sacrificial giving: *And do not be conformed to this world, but be transformed by the renewing of your mind, so that you may prove what the will of God is, that which is good and acceptable and perfect* (Romans 12:2).

REJOICE IN YOUR HEART

How did the Israelites respond when the fundraising for the temple was complete? They were beside themselves with joy: *Then the people rejoiced because they had offered so willingly, for they made their offering to the LORD with a whole heart, and King David also rejoiced greatly* (1 Chronicles 29:9). Maybe you have not yet arrived at the point of feeling happy, joyful, or blessed when you give, but that is exactly what God has in store for you when you practice generous giving. When you adopt God's giving nature, something wonderful will happen to your attitude, temperament, and spirit. God guarantees that you will become a joyful person when you become a generous giver.

RESERVE ETERNAL REWARDS

It is more blessed to give than to receive. Acts 20:35

If these first reasons are not enough, the fact that godly giving is rewarded is an exciting guarantee. Jesus emphasized the value of distinguishing between earthly and eternal rewards: *Do not store up for yourselves treasures upon earth, where moth and rust destroy, and where thieves break in and steal. But store up for yourselves treasures in heaven, where neither moth nor rust destroys, and where thieves do not break in or steal* (Matthew 6:19-20). Friend, you are reserving great stores of eternal rewards when you give generously.

RESTORE YOUR FELLOWSHIP WITH GOD

For where your treasure is, there your heart will be also. Matthew 6:21

Your heart follows your wallet. When you support what God is doing in the world around you and give to His causes, your heart will come into alignment with His. Your giving to His purposes will cause you to walk in partnership and fellowship with God.

Do you long to be closer to God? Ask Him what is on His heart. Look around you. Ask God where and what He wants you to give. As you develop the habit of partnering with God in your giving, any estrangement from Him you have been feeling will melt, giving way to intimacy and deep fellowship.

RELEASE GOD'S RESOURCES

Now it shall be, if you diligently obey the LORD your

*God, being careful to do all His commandments which
I command you today, the LORD your God will set
you high above all the nations of the earth. All these
blessings will come upon you and overtake you if you
obey the LORD your God.* Deuteronomy 28:1-2

Those who are godly givers often feel sorry for
those who do not give. They see that, due to fear and
unbelief, non-givers miss out on all the blessings God
has in store for them. If you diligently obey God in your
giving, blessing will come upon you and overtake you.
Malachi also says if we tithe diligently, God will pour out
a blessing from heaven for us until it *overflows* (Malachi
3:10). Not a bad return on your investment!

REVITALIZE YOUR LIFE

Growing in giving will inevitably stretch your
faith and your pocketbook, and you will find yourself
on your knees having deeper, more meaningful
conversations with the Almighty than you ever had
before. You will find your prayer life suddenly being
revitalized as you experience how God is going to bless
your finances. You will see how giving makes you focus
on others, strengthens your faith, and enriches your
prayer life. No longer will you search your brain for
something to talk to God about. You will be bursting with
good news: *The young lions do lack and suffer hunger;
but they who seek the LORD shall not be in want of any
good thing* (Psalm 34:10).

Giving also benefits your physical well-being.
Proverbs 3:7-8 instructs, *Do not be wise in your own
eyes; fear the LORD and turn away from evil. It will be
healing to your body and refreshment to your bones.*
As you turn away from stinginess toward God and
adopt a voluntary lifestyle of giving of yourself (your
time, money, and talents), you will experience overall
greater health. Financial insecurity breeds disease in

body, mind, and spirit. Stress and worry about material possessions cause all sorts of mental and physical health problems.

A study conducted on volunteerism by the Ontario Ministry of Health bears this out. Considering giving to be a voluntary act, the researchers found that participation in voluntary action does, indeed, contribute to the health, vitality, self-esteem, and longevity of volunteers. Volunteering can generate a heightened sense of self-worth and confidence, reduce heart rates and blood pressure, increase endorphin production (resulting in greater feelings of well-being and calm), boost immune system and nervous system functioning, reduce life's stresses, and overcome social isolation.[34]

In other words, those who cultivate a lifestyle of generosity and helping others report a greater sense of well-being, peace, community, and connection to family. They also tend to live longer than misers and hoarders. Which lifestyle do you choose?

RALLY OTHER CHRISTIANS

In 2 Corinthians 9:2, Paul makes an interesting statement about the Corinthians' readiness to give that tells us something about the inspiring effect godly givers have on others: *Your zeal has stirred up most of them.*

Let me tell you about someone who exemplifies this verse. A young lady and her family were trying to raise support for her Teen-Mania Mission Trip. They were working and praying as hard as they could to raise funds. Their congregation and even others outside their church were prompted by God to give generously. When she found there was an abundance of financial support over and beyond what she needed, she gave the leftover money to others trying to go on missions trips. These fellow believers were in turn strengthened and stirred in their faith. In the end, this young woman of God not only

---

34 - Graff, L. (1991). "Volunteer For The Health Of It." Etobicoke: Volunteer Ontario.

helped lead people to Christ on her mission trip, but her zeal stirred up faith in other Christian missionaries.

INCREASE YOUR GIVING CAPACITY

Since we have gifts that differ according to the grace given to us, each of us is to exercise them accordingly.
Romans 12:6

Health experts typically advise that an exercise regime include three phases: a few minutes of warm up, an extended period of strenuous activity, and then a brief cool down. In a similar fashion, it takes practice and commitment to learn the spiritual exercise of giving by faith.

As Christians learn to give their time, talents, and treasures to the Lord, they are able to trust Him at a certain capacity. Just as routine exercise brings increased health and physical ability, giving grows Christians' faith and increases their giving capacity and opportunities as they learn to trust God more and more with their resources.

BUILD RELATIONSHIPS

Some time ago, a friend of mine who had limited resources was able to buy an older home because he had a wealth of help from fellow believers. Christian givers helped with the down payment, painted ceilings, fixed bathrooms, restored patio awnings, laid carpet, and built fences around the property. Now, whenever my friend sees these improvements around his home he thinks of and prays for all those who helped him. Their generous giving deepened their relationship with him.

When you are in the act of giving, your heart is attuned to the Holy Spirit. He may bring to mind a rift in a particular relationship and may prompt you to go and make things right with that person:

*Therefore if you are presenting your offering at the
altar and there remember that your brother has
something against you, leave your offering there
before the altar, and go; first be reconciled to your
brother, and then come and present your offering.*
Matthew 5:23-24

A boyfriend or husband knows that flowers or
a special gift will smooth over rough waters and repair
a strained relationship with his sweetheart. We also
see in both the Old and New Testaments that giving
repairs relationships: *A gift in secret subdues anger*
(Proverbs 21:14). Giving can even close the gap between
believers and unbelievers: *I say to you, make friends for
yourselves by means of the wealth of unrighteousness;
so that when it fails, they may receive you into the
eternal dwellings* (Luke 16:9). In this parable, Jesus tells
believers to be as shrewd as unbelievers who understand
the power of money when it is used wisely. Ungodly
wealth used in a godly way will open both spiritual and
natural doors of opportunity and relationship.

PREVENT RECURRING MATERIALISM

One way to nip recurring materialism in the
bud is to give sacrificially when God prompts you. I'm
reminded of a couple that used to be visibly involved in
leadership in a small church, but over time they stopped
giving and attending regularly. Eventually they stopped
going and giving altogether, choosing to spend their
weekends traveling and enjoying other leisure activities.
They said they still listened to television evangelists and
read books on spiritual topics, but since they had "put in
their time and paid their dues," now it was time for them
to enjoy life.

There's nothing wrong with taking vacations
and enjoying retirement; however, taking vacations
from God and retiring from His kingdom will only

result in materialism and selfishness. This is why Jesus instructed, *Do not worry then, saying, "What will we eat?" or "What will we drink?" or "What will we wear for clothing?" For the Gentiles eagerly seek all these things; for your heavenly Father knows that you need all these things. But seek first His kingdom and His righteousness, and all these things will be added to you.* Matthew 6:31-33

THE OBSTACLE OF MATERIALISM

Few recognize that materialism is an obstacle to receiving the promises of God. They believe that one of the goals of living is to obtain "nice things." A big house, a more expensive car, or fancy jewelry – but the reality is that in chasing those things, people often become time-starved and physically, emotionally, and spiritually depleted.

The luxurious life is simply not very fulfilling. Seeking passionately after material things can be bad for the soul. Frequently, the quest for more things produces damaged relationships, a heightened risk of depression and anxiety, and less time for what truly makes us happy, like family, friendship, and being focused on others.

We are constantly bombarded by the television and other media with the mistaken message that things will make you happy. In fact, things can be an obstacle to the real gifts in life.

When we turn to material things to feel better, we instead compound the problem because we quickly discern that these things do not do a very good job of meeting our real needs. Even those who have achieved great wealth frequently find that a nagging appetite for bigger and better can never be satisfied. The passionate pursuit for more things is never-ending and can go on until death. We can always want more; that is usually not true of the real riches in life, such as quality friendships. With friends, we enjoy them but usually are not driven to need more and more of them. Instead, our nature is to pick out a few really good friends and then cultivate those friendships.

Stop chasing the things that cannot satisfy the soul! When people spend their effort pursuing material goods in the belief that they will bring happiness, they miss the biblical path of satisfaction and contentment. We think money will bring lots of happiness for a long time, but it normally brings us a little happiness for a short time.

THE BLESSINGS OF BEING FOCUSED ON OTHERS

Every year when Christmas comes, Christians remind themselves, in the midst of a commercial media barrage to the contrary, that "Jesus is the reason for the season." And then, joining with the rest of the nation, many still make the holiday about getting gifts. Of course, there is nothing wrong with getting and giving gifts as long as the focus and the truth of Christ remains and we remember the Gift that cost the Giver everything, the gift of a Savior.

Christmas forces us to experience contrasting behaviors:

1) We praise God for the birth of our Savior.

2) We scramble to shop and then delight in all the loot. Let's be honest, how many of our post-Christmas conversations begin with, "What did you get for Christmas?"

Christmas illustrates how the obstacle of materialism tries to rob us of the blessings God wants to flow into our lives as we walk on the real truth behind Christmas: Jesus came as a human being, determined to bless us by giving His life so that we may live!

To the degree that we are able to overcome the obstacle of being self-centered and walk in the biblical principle of blessing others, we unlock God's joy and blessings in our lives. Life is not about the things we accumulate; it is about the ones we bless.

Not only should we have an atmosphere of giving and service during the Christmas season, but we need to strive to walk in the biblical principles every day of the year. Throughout the year, on a daily basis, look for opportunities to have an attitude and awareness to bless others. Look for those in need and do what you can: buy groceries, paint a porch, spend time reading to a sick person, or just mow someone's lawn. Start to walk in the sacred things of God!

Has someone lost a job or a loved one? Or are they simply alone? Keep them in mind; make the needs of others your focus. Sometimes effective tactics are fairly simple. A blessing does not need to be cash or groceries – it can be time and commitment to a relationship, such as writing a handwritten note of encouragement or appreciation to someone you know. One of the sacred byproducts of a life centered on others is creativity, asking the Holy Spirit how you can give creatively of your resources to someone else, especially to those who may feel a bit forgotten.

There are countless "others-centered" opportunities each day. You will have no problem finding children in a family who need warm clothes, a food bank that needs help, or a neighbor who could use a kind word. Ask the Holy Spirit to help you care for the needs of others, defeating greed and any obstacle to becoming generous and blessing those around you. The pure act of giving in Jesus' name jolts even the jaded.

God wants us to freely enjoy the gifts we receive

in the same way that our heavenly Father wants us to enjoy the wonderful and amazing gifts bestowed upon us by Him. Tithe biblical principle here is that we all should strive to keep our focus on others to move their hearts and minds of others toward Jesus Christ - the greatest gift ever given to mankind.

Imagine you are a soda can God has filled with ideas for giving, but something has kept you sealed up. What is holding you back?

Recently, a friend's son inadvertently gave me a great illustration of how God can expand what we have and make it powerful. Reaching into a cooler, this young man took out a can of grape soda and vigorously shook it, then punctured a small hole in the metal dimple next to the pop-top.

Clearly, he planned to drink the soda quickly! But before he could get the can to his mouth, the purple fizz shot up to the ceiling and all over the chandelier and the walls of his family's dining room. His parents came in just as the can erupted in all its glory. Once the sticky spray started, it was difficult to stop without being caught in its crossfire. The can had to expend its energy before the family could go about the business of cleaning up the mess.

I have thought about this scene several times (with a smile), and I realize that giving to God is a lot like that incident with the grape soda. God fills our heads with bubbling ideas of where and how to give. These ideas excite us but may seem insignificant in the world's economy. We may feel we have nothing more than a soda-can measure of influence, but even a small step in giving can unleash God's power. The fun is in seeing it spill out and expand to cover more and more territory. In order for our money to become pressed down, shaken together, and poured out, we need to learn how we acquire the mindset of giving in the first place. Jesus tells us that generous stewardship begins in us when our hearts are pressed into God's image. Luke 6:27-38 says:

But I say to you who hear, love your enemies, do good to those who hate you, bless those who curse you, pray for those who mistreat you. Whoever hits you on the cheek, offer him the other also; and whoever takes away your coat, do not withhold your shirt from him either. Give to everyone who asks of you, and whoever takes away what is yours, do not demand it back. Treat others the same way you want them to treat you. If you love those who love you, what credit is that to you? For even sinners love those who love them. If you do good to those who do good to you, what credit is that to you? For even sinners do the same. If you lend to those from whom you expect to receive, what credit is that to you? Even sinners lend to sinners in order to receive back the same amount. But love your enemies, and do good, and lend expecting nothing in return; and your reward will be great, and you will be sons of the Most High; for He Himself is kind to ungrateful and evil men. *Be merciful, just as your Father is merciful. Do not judge, and you will not be judged; and do not condemn, and you will not be condemned; pardon, and you will be pardoned. Give, and it will be given to you. They will pour into your lap a good measure - pressed down, shaken together, and running over. For by your standard of measure it will be measured to you in return.*

When I give, I will receive back *good measure.* What does this mean? In the Greek, "good" is kalos, which means, "beauty, completeness, balance, or proportion."[35] Who would not want goodness given to them in their area of greatest need? "Measure," or metron, means in this context "to capacity." In other words, what I give is going to be given back to me at full capacity, all I can handle. "Pressed down" means "to force down, to make room for more," and "shaken together" means "to sift that which you press down so there is room."[36] Last, I must ask what it is that will be measured to me in return. The answer: whatever I invest in. What I give is what I will receive.

Think for a moment what the text is saying. It

35 - Zodhiates, S. (1992).
36 - ibid

is making what seems to be a contradictory promise: by giving, we will have more. God will often offend the mind in order to reveal the heart: *Because the foolishness of God is wiser than men, and the weakness of God is stronger than men* (1 Corinthians 1:25). What this means in real life is that if I am feeling lonely, the Bible promises I will feel better if I give attention to someone who is perhaps lonelier than I. If I am short of money, I should give some away; God promises it will return in even greater measure than I gave. This is God's reward for godly givers. This is His promise.

Many seemingly illogical biblical instructions are foundations of our faith. Does it make sense to confess your sin or pray to someone you cannot even see? Does it make sense that you become a leader by serving? Does it make sense to read a book written two thousand years ago by a number of different authors in multiple languages over several centuries, and allow that book's message to change your life?

Much of what we believe is simply on the basis of faith. And much of what we believe we have to put into practice. We believe God's promise about giving, and we act on it. This is our faith.

In the passage from Luke 6, "great reward" can be translated as "rich, strong, intense, and abundant."[37] Not only does a godly giver receive great rewards but he or she also gains a great relationship with the Most High.

The same measure with which we portion out blessings or confer money to others in need will be used to measure back to us when we are in need. If we give in stinginess, stinginess will be measured back to us. If we give lavishly, lavish giving will be measured back to us. As one friend of mine likes to say, "Whatever we spoon out to give to God, He will spoon out to give back to us. And He's got a much bigger spoon."

---

37 - Zodhiates, S. (1992).

Christian, give your life and your service to the Lord. Trust that His promises are true and follow His principles. In return, your reward will be the joy of seeing His work accomplished throughout the world and a personal life of rich, strong, intense abundance and joy far exceeding anything you could ever imagine. When you think of these benefits to God's work and to our lives, how could you not give?

Whatever has held you back from giving like you should in the past, today is a new day, a new opportunity to decide what you will do with the resources God has provided for you. What will your decision be?

/ **Conclusion**